The
Renewal of
The Ministry

The
Renewal of
The Ministry

THOMAS J. MULLEN

**With an Introduction by
D. Elton Trueblood**

Abingdon Press

NASHVILLE
NEW YORK

THE RENEWAL OF THE MINISTRY

Copyright © 1963 by Abingdon Press

ISBN 0-687-36151-6

Library of Congress Catalog Card Number: 63-14596

Scripture quotations unless otherwise noted
are from the Revised Standard Version of the
Bible, copyrighted 1946 and 1952 by the Divi-
sion of Christian Education, National Council
of Churches, and are used by permission.

Quotations from *The New English Bible* are
© The Delegates of the Oxford University
Press and The Syndics of The Cambridge
University Press 1961.

MANUFACTURED BY THE PARTHENON PRESS AT
NASHVILLE, TENNESSEE, UNITED STATES OF AMERICA

To NANCY

Introduction

ANY PERSON WHO CARES ABOUT THE CHRISTIAN CAUSE IS BOUND to be deeply concerned about the ministry. Those on the front lines in the major spiritual and moral struggles of our time are undoubtedly the lay people, but the lay people are not likely to make an effective witness unless they are guided, instructed, and inspired by those engaged in a vital ministry. Whenever we discover something new and exciting in the church we always find that, in the midst of it, there is a *man*. It is men who make the difference and some of the men who are most effective in our total civilization are those whose lives are dedicated to the public or professional ministry. The Christian ideal is that of the universal or lay ministry, but this ideal cannot be realized unless there are men who specialize in making it real.

Important as the ministry is, it is full of problems. Thousands of pastors are puzzled or even frustrated men. Frequently they discover that the picture of their role which led originally to their vocational decision bears little resemblance to what occurs in fact. They find that the general public, and even the lay members, look upon them as belonging to a class apart, that they are expected to be official holy men, saying the pious words on ceremonial occasions, and that their success is measured primarily by how many people they can persuade to listen to them on Sunday morning. More than most human beings the pastor is flattered to his face and criticized behind his back. His temptations, both to pride and to despair, are more intense than those of most men.

The immense merit of Thomas Mullen's book is his clear recognition that the central problem which faces the minister is that of his own identity. It is hard for him, in the midst of competing and even contradictory pressures, to know who he is. This basic problem must be solved before lesser problems can be rightly stated. Is he prophet, teacher, promoter, performer, preacher, counselor, visitor, business manager, or what? This question is not easy to answer because it is intrinsically complex. Thomas Mullen approaches it with a recognition of its complexity and with a forthright honesty that is refreshing. Because he is free from romantic illusions about the ministry, he is not shocked at the pattern which others seek to impose upon his life, and because he sees that any known alternative to a pastoral system would be worse, he is not seriously tempted to abandon his calling.

I have seen this book grow from its early form to its present maturity, and I am deeply pleased with the outcome. I know of no book in print which deals with the central issues of the character of the ministry in such a combination of realism and hope. It should have a wide reading, not merely among ministers, but also among lay men and women who are searching for the right pattern of recovery.

Almost any task that does not harm human life can be justified with a little effort, but there are a few tasks which require no justification because they are self-authenticating. The ministry of Jesus Christ is clearly one of these. It involves great dangers, and sometimes it leads to agony of spirit, but it is always very close to greatness. Sometimes genuine greatness appears, but it never appears unless the minister knows who he is, and unless those whom he serves know this also. Thomas Mullen's book is calculated to aid in the answer to this question.

D. ELTON TRUEBLOOD

Preface

THIS BOOK ORIGINALLY BEGAN AS AN EFFORT TO DESCRIBE THE image of the Quaker pastor, under the sponsorship of the Board on Christian Vocations of the Five Years Meeting of the Society of Friends. However, because the Quaker pastor has largely appropriated the general Protestant conception of the pastor for himself, it immediately became apparent that the effort should be broader in scope. The ministry in nearly every denomination shares most of the deficiencies—and most of the virtues—of the pastoral system in the Society of Friends, and no single Christian group has a monopoly on either its virtues or its vices.

I have not sought here to appeal for a return to *the* New Testament ministry, even though I am convinced that the ministry herein described is congenial with the spirit, and frequently the letter, of the New Testament. What I want to provide is an understanding of the ministry that has a relevance for our time. The same situation confronting our day did not obtain in the first century. There was no church on the corner,

11

no theological seminary, no denominations, and no rivalry between large ecclesiastical promotional bodies.

What ought the ministry to be now? We cannot get along with it as it now functions, but neither can we get along without it. This book is an effort to see where we are now and to describe the direction in which we ought to be going in the pastoral ministry.

Since it is a first book, there is a great temptation to express lengthy personal feelings of gratitude and affection for many people who have influenced the author's life, beginning with parents and including a great variety of other persons who have offered helpful suggestions. For the most part, however, this temptation will have to be resisted simply because there are too many to whom I am indebted.

A word of thanks must be given, however, to some whose guidance and help have spared the reader from several weaknesses the original manuscript contained. Wesley Shrader, my former teacher at Yale Divinity School, must be remembered because of his help in some of my early writing efforts. Wayne Booth, former chairman of the English Department at Earlham College and now the Pullman Professor of English at the University of Chicago, read the entire manuscript and patiently corrected many of the errors of expression and conception I would not have made had I paid closer attention when I was a student in his classes. Elton Trueblood merits my greatest appreciation, however, for his continual interest and help in writing this book. He has demonstrated again and again in our relationship the remarkable ability to be critical of my ideas but tender with me as a person. A next-to-last word of appreciation should be directed toward the members of the Quaker community in New Castle, Indiana, who have taught me, by example, many of the things that the churches ought to be doing.

Among them, special thanks is due Glen McGrew who typed most of the manuscript.

The final word, as usual, must go to Nancy who, as an understanding wife, allowed me to share the joys of our two daughters while sparing me from most of their demands. Were she not who she is, no book would have been written.

T. J. M.

Contents

chapter 1

The Predicament of the Ministry

*If we could first know where we were,
and whither we are tending, we could
better judge what to do, and how to
do it.*   —ABRAHAM LINCOLN

THE PROTESTANT MINISTRY IS SICK. THERE IS NOT LIKELY TO BE
a real renewal of the Christian Church without a vital ministry,
but the trouble is that the ministry, which should be a cure for
the lethargy and confusion which plagues the church, itself re-
sembles the disease.

A primary symptom of the sickness is the fact that young
men and women in the 1960's are not entering the pastoral
ministry in anything like sufficient numbers. In nearly every
Protestant denomination the current complaint is the same:
there aren't enough pastors to fill pulpits. There aren't even
enough men to meet high priority needs, much less enough
men to satisfy the needs of new churches and the expanding
ministry of large churches which are growing larger. Even a
cursory glance at available statistics clearly demonstrates this
fact. The United Presbyterian Church, the Protestant Epis-

17

copal Church, The Methodist Church, and the United Lutheran Church have all discovered a serious shortage in the number of men and women needed to fill pulpits in their denominations.[1]

The problem is general and is not, therefore, the special concern of any particular denomination. It touches every major Protestant group in this country, and it is a problem that may very well get worse before it gets any better.

The natural reaction of concerned people is to ask why. Why is it that in the past few years the pastoral ministry has been decreasingly attractive to high-school and college graduates? Why is it that many young men and women who have the "right" motives, namely, the desire to serve and an eagerness to improve our society, do not end up as pastors in American communities?

Certainly many considerations enter into the answer, some old and some new. It is true that among the "professions" the pastoral ministry is relatively non-lucrative. The kind of person, by and large, who makes the best pastor also makes the best doctor, teacher, and lawyer—and these other professions pay more. However, these professions, too, are finding themselves shorthanded, so the answer cannot be that they are siphoning off more than their share of the eligible and eager young men and women. We know, also, that there is less deep interest today in local religion than there has been in the past. Some have probably concluded, too, that one does not have to be a clergyman in order to minister, and many potential pastors are expressing their religious impulses through worthy and related Christian vocations such as social work, YMCA leadership, and humanitarian service.

[1] Louis Cassels, "Churches Facing Pastor Famine," *The Indianapolis News*, Jan. 27, 1961; see also Gereon Zimmermann, "Help Wanted: Ministers, Priests and Rabbis," *Look* magazine, Nov. 20, 1962, pp. 112-20.

John Wiclein, writing for the *New York Times* in April, 1961, suggested this reason for the shortage:

The kind of dedication demanded by the ministry is now demanded by science. The nation's plea for scientists since sputnik went into orbit in 1957 has "called" many who would otherwise be entering seminaries. Science has almost been made a religion of its own, particularly by philosopher physicists relating it to the ethical problems.

That fewer men are entering the ministry is obvious, but there is the real possibility, too, that there is a *qualitative* shortage of men as well. Some colleges, in fact, frankly admit that their preministerial students are not of the highest caliber. Of all the finalists, for example, in the recent National Merit Scholarships Fund, only 3 per cent of the men wanted religious careers. More than half of these elite declared for the physical sciences.[2]

However, we are probably wrong if we seek to solve the problem by competing more intensely for the highly motivated young person. Better methods of recruitment, more scholarship aid, and more efforts to convince young people that they ought to go into the pastoral ministry may increase the number of seminarians, but these attempts will not get at the real answer. There has always been keen competition from many fields for the best young people. The fact is, in other words, that when we merely "work harder" to compete, we are treating the symptom rather than the disease itself.

The essence of the problem is the meaning of the pastoral ministry. The ministry itself is not hale and hearty, and until this fact is taken seriously, a vital and dynamic ministry will not appear to stimulate the Christian cause which now lies

[2] Zimmermann, *op. cit.*, p. 120.

dormant. To many, what it means to be a local pastor is badly confused. The mental picture of what Protestant pastors do between sermons is vague and unclear. It is true that some few Americans now think that the pastor does nothing but preach, marry, bury, and baptize. Others know that he is "busy," but they are not really sure what he is busy doing or what his business is. The image of the physician or the lawyer or the teacher or the research chemist is sharp and clear. The image of a Protestant pastor between Monday and Saturday is fuzzy and confused.

However, there is good reason to think that the fuzziness of the image is itself another symptom of the sickness of the ministry. While what it means to be a Protestant pastor may be unclear, it seems obvious that there is an *impression* being felt by young men and women which has very real connotations. Potential pastors, in other words, may be uncertain as to what they *see* in the pastoral ministry, but they know they are uncomfortable about what they *feel* is involved in it.

Because Christian sociologists and theologians have been concerned about both the confusion and the impression of the image for several years, a number of efforts have been made to pin down the roles and purpose of the Protestant pastor.[3] Some have attempted to eliminate the confusion that has existed even in the minds of seminary teachers, and to a large degree they have succeeded, although their findings have not been taken seriously enough by either seminaries or local churches. However, as the image becomes clearer, so does the reason for the

[3] Perhaps the most important of these is H. Richard Niebuhr's classic study, *The Purpose of the Church and Its Ministry* (New York: Harper & Row, 1956). Especially helpful to this author has been Edwin L. Becker's unpublished doctoral dissertation, entitled *Religious Field Work as Experience in the Social Roles of the Minister*, 1956. A shorter article, more widely distributed, is "A Young Minister's Dilemma," *The Christian Century*, April 25, 1956, pp. 508-10, by Samuel W. Blizzard. *The Ministry*, Richard Spann, Editor (Nashville: Abingdon Press, 1949), also has several helpful chapters on this subject.

vague dissatisfaction with the confused picture of the Protestant pastor which so many potential ministers have felt. When we are able to understand what the Christian ministry ought to be, therefore, we are able to go beyond the symptoms of sickness in the ministry and examine the disease itself.

One of the main centers of infection is the fact that the role of the pastor is shaped more by the expectations of the people than by biblical, theological, and even historical truths. The local congregation, local and national mores, caricatures in fiction and journalism, and sometimes irrelevant traditions have produced a pastoral ministry which is in conflict with a biblical and theological understanding at point after point. The Protestant ministry must share the judgment which has frequently—and rightly—been made of Christianity as a whole, namely, that it reflects and embraces the society in which it lives, when it ought to be judging and reforming that society. In other words, Christianity and the American way of life, or Christianity and "common decency" have become synonymous in the minds of thousands of church members. Unfortunately, too, the actions and attitudes of ministers force us to conclude that the identification has been made by them as well. Those who should be the doctors for the sickness of Christianity have themselves caught the disease.

Ministers and their churches often share, for example, a decidedly "worldly" vision of success. When eager and idealistic young men in college and seminary look forward to the pastoral ministry, they see as their purpose to preach the gospel and increase the love of man for God and for his neighbor. In actual fact, however, they soon learn that the purpose of the local church is something else. They learn that the purpose of the church—and consequently of the minister—is to get big crowds out to meetings. The successful minister is the man who is pastor of a large church.

A pertinent example of this distortion is made by an advertisement which appeared in a magazine on preaching subscribed to by thousands of top-flight ministers. The advertisement was titled, "Filling Empty Pews the Parish Paper Way," and included the following paragraphs:

Did you ever feel the thrill a pastor experiences when his church is moving ahead rapidly, money is pouring into the treasury, church packed at every meeting, and a nice crowd out at the mid-week service?

Do you know that if you are going to be a success as a church manager you must take advantage of modern church methods? Are you aware of the fact that nearly all progressive ministers publish parish papers? A parish paper competes with the movies, the automobile, the Sunday newspaper, with golf, and beats them decisively. A parish paper fills empty pews and keeps them filled.

Notice, please, the assumptions of this advertisement. When is a church moving ahead rapidly? When people and money come into the church. How is a pastor to get people into the church? By competing with the movies, the automobile, the Sunday newspaper, and golf. What is a progressive pastor? One who uses this gimmick and, presumably, other gimmicks like it. Remember, too, that this advertisement appeared in a magazine subscribed to by ministers, and it is undoubtedly written with the impression that many ministers (and potential customers) will accept its assumptions.

A pastor does not have to serve a church very long to discover that these assumptions are held by many other members besides those in the parish paper business. How many times as he walks down the street does he meet one of his congregation who almost immediately offers what could be called the "automatic apology": "Say, Reverend Jones, I'm sorry I wasn't in church last Sunday, but . . ." He assumes, in other words, that the primary matter a minister is concerned with is whether or not people made it "out" to a public meeting or a service. It is difficult, of course, to know whether this standard of success is the result of the expectations of the people or of the pastor. Elton Trueblood does not mince words when he comments on this situation in a recent book:

> The paradox of the apparent victory, yet real defeat, of the contemporary Church is nowhere more vividly demonstrated than in the present concentration upon *attendance*. Great billboard advertisements appear by the hundreds with a single message, "Worship Together This Week." The fact that the donors of the advertisement are undoubtedly motivated by goodwill toward the life of religion, as they understand it, does not obscure the fundamental ineptitude of their effort. Obviously, the sponsors of the advertisements look upon attendance at a religious assembly as the major religious act or the major evidence of church membership. It is no wonder that they think this, if they observe the frantic and sometimes ingenious efforts of pastors, week by week, to surpass all previous records of attendance.[4]

The point is that attendance records are a non-biblical and essentially non-Christian standard of success. Yet they represent the accepted mark of religious achievement—along with huge budgets—of the contemporary church *and its pastor.*

The contemporary pastor also reflects the expectations of our society in the methods he uses to achieve the standards of success which have been grafted on to the church from its society. The "Parish Paper Way" illustrates both wrong ends and wrong means, and it is not difficult to find numerous other examples as well. Dr. George W. Crane, whose versatile column "The

[4] D. Elton Trueblood, *The Company of the Committed* (New York: Harper & Row, 1961), pp. 18-19.

Worry Clinic" is avidly read by hundreds of thousands several times each week, presupposes the acceptability of methods which are not necessarily appropriate for Christian ministers. In Case E-406 a seminary student asks for a prescription for becoming "a live-wire in the pulpit to electrify a congregation." Dr. Crane assumes at the outset that such clergymen "have sincere devotion and religious idealism." However, his column is primarily concerned with the psychological strategy by which "a clergyman can double attendance, win far more converts, and even zoom his salary." Among his suggestions are these:

Remember names and faces. It inflates the ego of parishioners to have their priest or clergyman call them by name. . . . Name at least 3 parishioners in your sermon every Sunday, but do this in an incidental but complimentary manner. . . . Urge classes to divide into teams with a Captain over each. Schedule short contests of a monthly nature, with the winning team to be entertained at a picnic or wiener roast by the losers. . . . A preacher should praise those who placed flowers on the altar, as well as the ushers, singers, and especially the cooks for the church suppers. . . . Harness youth as by encouraging rewards for children who memorize Bible verses. And use the young folks for surveys of church attendance and to publish mimeographed papers.[5]

Dr. Crane offers the minister several gimmicks which can magnify his influence. Evidently he feels that flattery will get the young preacher somewhere, and evidently he assumes that if the pastor wants to "double attendance" and "zoom his salary" the way to do it is to build up the egos of his parishioners. Once the standard of success (big crowds, big budgets) has been assumed, methods of achieving success (flattery, gimmicks) can also be assumed.

In a more scholarly analysis of this situation, Martin Marty

[5] Dr. George W. Crane, "The Worry Clinic," Case E-406. Used by permission of The Hopkins Syndicate, Inc.

has arrived at a provocative and straightforward answer as to what is wrong with these methods:

It is probably proper to boast that Beloved Disciple Church mauled the Prince of Peace basketball team, as the sportswriters put it, and to allow for a bit of semispiritual gamesmanship. But every religious group can provide ample evidence that the success stories of parishes are usually told with a different end in view: *they absolutize the competitive principle at the expense of vital Christian motivations and means*[6] [italics mine].

The minister himself has come to accept uncritically the expectations of society that his role is a kind of "catch-all," a hodge-podge of activities that have a distant connection with goodness, piety, and Christianity. This is why the ministerial role is so confused. Different social influences have charged the pastor with such a wide variety of functions and duties that his weekly agenda features a baffling array of activities that he *assumes* are his to perform. Nearly every minister has too many bosses and wears too many hats. It is true that every minister will have to wear more than one hat; he cannot be *only* a preacher or counselor or teacher. However, he dare not spread himself too thin. He has to know himself and choose priorities in his work from among the myriad of activities, jobs, chores, and duties which confront him daily. *What he is* must be reasonably clear, else the minister's role becomes a floating target that is at the mercy of cultural pressures and irrelevant demands. The problem is analogous to that of finding a place in the company for the boss's son. No one knows exactly what his job is, and as a consequence he is placed in the insecure position of doing whatever little jobs are tossed his way. Neither

[6] Martin Marty, *The New Shape of American Religion* (New York: Harper & Row, 1959), p. 128.

he nor the minister, it seems, has a real function, or a vital responsibility.

A recent magazine article, which really was about the minister's wife, showed rather clearly the unfortunate condition of the Protestant pastorate:

> During a marathon working day, a minister is required to serve as a no-fee psychoanalyst, group therapist, marriage counselor, scoutmaster, civic leader, fund raiser, Rotary luncheon speaker, bookkeeper, administrator, mimeograph machine technician, public-relations expert, typist, and even gardener, janitor, and plumber. When he has a free minute, he prepares his sermon and the order of his Sunday services.

> The new-time clergyman, in short, is a spiritual handyman, a salesman, a servant, and a religious "organization man." Yet he does not really belong anywhere except in the church—and this in a society that demands churchmen to be more worldly than ever before. . . . That is . . . why a "pulpit committee" casting about for a new minister often scrutinizes the wife as carefully as a big corporation looks over the wives of potential executives.[7]

The author, probably with the majority of Americans, assumes that it is society which "demands" that the minister perform certain functions and be a certain kind of person. Why the ministry is sick can be seen by analyzing the above list of roles which the minister is "required" to perform. Of them, only the counselor or therapist role is particularly appealing, at least to dedicated men. How about the others? Will men of devotion, enthusiasm, and a sense of a "holy call" be eager to become a "spiritual handyman, a salesman, a servant, and a religious organization man?" Would you be?

[7] From *The New Time Religion* by Claire Cox. Copyright © 1961 by Claire Cox. Published by Prentice-Hall, Inc.

The fundamental criticism of this picture of the Protestant minister is serious. Not only does it hinder and confuse the religious purpose of the church, it attracts the wrong kind of men to the ministry. When we come right down to it, will Madison Avenue techniques and Madison Avenue technicians really meet the needs of people? Is modern man hungry for more gimmicks, or is he hungry for a sense of purpose and meaning in his life? If ministers assume that they are to do whatever menial or trivial chore comes their way, will they be able to revitalize the Christianity of our day that is in retreat and in serious danger of losing its distinctive witness?

If the Bible and the history of the Christian church is right, the answer is clearly "no." It is a "no" which comes from persons who might be attracted to a different kind of ministry, like one student who rejected the parish ministry and gave this reason: "If to be a minister is to be merely a solicitor of funds, or a general psychiatrist, or an organizer of Bingo parties, if to be a minister is to be merely a unit of a social machine—then I believe the ordained ministry is not for me." [8]

In actuality the Protestant ministry has deserted a basic truth which the Reformation fathers made clear. That truth is simply that the Christian religion cannot be practiced by a special group *for* another group. Christian faith is a matter of personal devotion, personal relationship to God, and personal living for all Christians—not by a few, not by the specially trained, and certainly not by those professionally paid for the job. Yet, due to the expectations by our society for the ministerial role, an actual retreat to a pre-Reformation meaning of ministry has largely taken place. One scholar describes a major role of the Protestant minister to be that of the "religious representative."

[8] Zimmermann, *op. cit.*, p. 117.

The minister is expected to be the promoter of religion and of his particular church. He is valued as a minister in proportion to his ability to attract people to him and consequently to the church. In a day when personality is greatly emphasized, ministers with pleasant and winning personalities are in demand. The minister must not even unconsciously alienate people from himself since he would then be serving as a poor representative of religion and the church.[9]

A subtle but important shift in the thinking of Protestants is involved here. Emphasis upon personal faith by all Christians is overlooked as Christians concentrate on the personality and image of the pastor who, it seems, is the embodiment of religion. He represents the congregation. He stands for religion. In a very real sense the Protestant pastor is expected to reflect or represent religion for, or in place of, a congregation. And the minister had better be a proper representative, too, in terms of the social and economic expectations of his congregation.

For example, personal appearance makes a tremendous difference to a clientele—in this case a congregation—in the pastoral ministry. If a pastor is extremely liberal or extremely conservative in his theology, he may—just may—get into trouble with his congregation. But God help him if he has bad breath, or wears dirty shirts, or loud socks! The local pastor is expected to drive a car that is appropriate to the economic level of his church. He must make a certain number of public appearances at the "right" gatherings. He represents religion. Rather, he represents a group of people who probably have similiar economic standards, mores, and a sense of pride in their institutional image.

A few years ago Murray Leiffer made a detailed and com-

[9] Edwin Becker, *op. cit.*, pp. 83 ff.

prehensive study of what Methodist laymen wanted and expected in their pastors. Among the questions he asked were several that had to do with personal matters. The composite answer that was returned was clear.[10] A minister would not be acceptable if (1) he is greatly overweight, (2) untidy in his personal appearance, (3) enjoys wearing flashy or sporty clothes outside the pulpit, (4) has bad breath or noticeable body odor, (5) is not punctual in meeting his engagements, (6) is lax in meeting his financial obligations, and (7) occasionally loses control of his temper.

We do not mean to suggest that these matters are unimportant or that a minister is a better minister with bad breath than without. In fairness we may even grant that the general hope, probably, of those who answered the questionnaire was for a minister who is not stuffy and distant, who demonstrates warmth and a genuine interest in them. The point we want to make is simply that too much emphasis is placed upon such matters as these, while too little is paid to what a minister believes and the interpretation of the gospel he brings. A real "nice fellow" with a colorful personality will be regarded as a better pastor than a drab personality with a good theology. After all, one's frayed shirt cuffs will cast one's church into disrepute faster than one's poorly thought-out conception of God.

Later in Leiffer's book he quotes a statement from one layman who summarizes the qualifications of "the minister the laymen want":

In my personal opinion a preacher should try to use the Bible in preaching; try to keep out of the ruts and keep improving himself; do his best for the young people; keep the old pets in good humor;

[10] Murray H. Leiffer, *The Layman Looks at the Minister* (Nashville: Abingdon Press, 1947), pp. 159-60.

be cheerful, optimistic; tell the truth; mix with the whole town; enter civic endeavors; pay his debts; be a good student of human nature; regard the church as holy ground; have spiritual services; know his members; and use his judgment in visiting.[11]

The question the potential pastor faces when confronted by this image is a real one. He wonders: "Does the service of God mean that I should keep the old pets in good humor? Is the role of a minister so nebulous and confused that it is part of my job to tell the truth, pay my debts, and be cheerful?" Surely we want doctors, lawyers, clerks, and Indian chiefs to pay their debts, be cheerful, and tell the truth. Yet, we do not normally regard these matters as part of their task. The role of "figurehead" does not inspire men of dedication and concern. It causes them to hesitate and possibly to retreat.

The well-dressed, neatly groomed religious representative must also be able to make a proper prayer, and he especially must be able to give a proper banquet invocation. If we were, in fact, to name one of the primary twentieth-century phenomena of the Protestant faith, it would have to be the nearly universal assumption that only pastors can pray. God, it seems, cannot hear a layman's public prayer. It is assumed that if a pastor is present he will be hurt if not asked to pray or "say a few words" or demonstrate his "expertness" in some other way. Ask almost any busy minister for his daily or weekly agenda, and it will undoubtedly include one, two, or more occasions which he is expected to attend in order to pray or invoke or bless. Sometimes the occasions for expert praying are unusual, as was the case of a minister who was asked to travel out to a country field to give an invocation at a kite-flying contest. Usually, however, professional praying is done at such routine gatherings

11 *Ibid.,* pp. 137-38.

as church suppers service clubs, Boy Scout meetings, the opening of Little League, or special co-operative religious functions in the city.

The minister is expected to use a special vocabulary and certain religious phrases. When a minister stands to speak, he is expected to say certain things, be for certain things, and be opposed to certain other things. The people present listen, but they do not listen closely because they assume that what the minister has to say is of little interest to them. Just as most of what taxidermists have to say is of actual interest only to other taxidermists, what the religious representative has to say is of interest only to other religious representatives. By and large this distortion of the pastoral role is not completely the fault of the pastor, as the words he uses and the points he makes are probably true and possibly relevant. However, the misunderstanding of the pastor's task at this point has suffered from the misunderstanding of the Christian religion as a whole. The religious representative, in other words, is somewhat irrelevant because Christianity is somewhat irrelevant. Once again this kind of ministry is too often observed to be ignored. It is there, and young men interested in the pastoral ministry must either be discouraged by it or attempt to transcend it.

The sickness of the ministry is compounded, too, by the fact that sugar pills are being passed off as real medicine. The minister usually thinks of himself as a critic of society, and, in a very general sense, public expectations also include the prophetic or reforming role. Yet real criticism that can be taken seriously is not usually offered from American pulpits, or if it is, the "prophet" finds himself frustrated. In every community there are social evils against which the pastor should preach, and most people in the church will agree that these wrongs do exist. However, while there may be awareness, there is usually no concern. The minister is frustrated, precisely because the rightness or wrongness of his stand makes little difference. He may be able to justify his position in terms of scripture, theology, common sense, an appeal to conscience, or the dusty canons of his denominational history. So what? If the timid criticisms he makes seem to be directed toward those institutions that contain members of his congregation, his words will not be heard. Some will even punish the pastor by not attending *his* services. A few will have him investigated. If he insists upon trying to apply the gospel to real life, he may be visited by a committee and counseled. One minister in his private conversations made clear his political feelings, which happened to be different from the majority of his congregation. He was not only visited and "counseled," he was accused of being a Communist and has since received anonymous and threatening phone calls. This is an extreme case, but it indicates the kind of frustration the reformer can expect.

Stanley Rowland, Jr., stated this point very well in an article in the *Nation* some time ago. In speaking of the religious problems of suburbia, he wrote: "The Holy Ghost had better stay ghostly and the preacher platitudinous, for sermons must console, comfort, inspire to pleasant living—but not challenge the suburbanite with the rude realities of today's revolutionary world." [12] For the man who can recognize a platitude when he sees one, the pressure to be platitudinous may be more than he wants to resist. One wonders if the pastor is discouraged more by the inevitable unpopularity that will come with real prophetism or by the general awareness of his ineffectiveness as a prophet.

Many, of course, do not resist the pressure and merely give in to the expectations of their society. Robert Raines in his book *New Life in the Church* illustrates this vividly:

[12] Stanley Rowland, Jr., *The Nation*, July 28, 1956.

In a recent conference on human relations, a church leader was asked what the church ought to do in the problem of race relations. The reply was: "Well, we can't go any faster than our laymen." This appears harmless. But, in fact, it is a way of saying: "If the will of our people and the will of God are in conflict, we shall do the will of the people." [13]

Will the man who wants to go faster than his people enter the ministry? Or will he, like so many others, join the rat race of people working for financial security and abdicate the responsibility which his conscience has put upon him? Or will he continue to seek a place where he can give his reforming desire and abilities practical expression—as in social work, refugee programs, or the Peace Corps?

Eager and idealistic young people want to change the world, or at least help change it, for the better. A ministry in which prophets boldly make their witness, proclaiming fearlessly "Thus saith the Lord . . . ," preaching Truth, Justice, and Righteousness, leading concerned men and women against the evils of society—this kind of ministry is a cure for the sickness of the church and for itself. However, this kind of ministry is infrequently observed in Christian churches today. Instead of being a voice crying in the wilderness, the Protestant ministry has demonstrated itself to be a whisper lost in the wind. The reformer only reforms when his words and his deeds are specific and objective. When the pastor preaches against badness, falsehood, the Devil, and Communism in Russia—in other words, general impersonal enemies—his message loses its reality. Chances are the alert and dedicated young men of our day will be repelled by this sight. They will be repelled, not because they think there are no such forces of evil in the world,

[13] Robert Raines, *New Life in the Church* (New York: Harper & Row, 1961), p. 17.

but because they think there are. Such young people may very well conclude that the place to fight evil concretely and specifically is somewhere outside the pastoral ministry, for within it, it seems, only *talk* about justice flows down like waters and *clichés* about righteousness like an ever-flowing stream.

The sickness has not killed the ministry nor its church *yet*. Within it are some who have managed to rise above the expectations of society and bring a legitimate and relevant ministry to the congregations they serve. You and I can think of such men and women. Possibly we have been influenced by them. We must never forget that while many young men are turning away from the pastoral ministry, many others are entering it who possibly heard a call first through the message and example of a significant man doing significant work.

However, this same logic leads us to conclude that many young men are turning away from the pastoral ministry because pastors of their experience seem to be insignificant persons doing insignificant work. The sobering fact is that the roles a pastor plays are far too frequently distorted. The legitimate work he does—or is supposed to do—is buried under a sea of menial chores, personal compromises, and irrelevant activities. Obviously, the work of the pastoral ministry can vary tremendously, but we must become awakened to the fact that the distorted role is coming to be regarded as normal. What the sincere and dedicated pastor wants to regard as the rule is becoming the exception. People are beginning to anticipate a stereotype that is basically unappealing to many potential ministers.

This is why the shortage of qualified men for the pastoral ministry is a symptom of our sickness. The stereotype of the pastor repels the kind of men who are desperately needed as the cure. A recent report from the presidents or academic deans of several of our leading seminaries emphasizes this fact. Martin

34

THE PREDICAMENT OF THE MINISTRY

Marty, in his analysis of the report in the *Christian Century*, made these observations:

[The majority felt that] great numbers of young people will seek vocations that provide a sense of mission and purpose in preference to more lucrative executive or research positions. Several were of the opinion that many college students had forsaken seminary precisely because they felt that greater purpose could be found elsewhere (in social work, the Peace Corps, etc.).

The overwhelming majority of the seminary heads [felt that] . . . underlying the whole problem, however, was [this reason]: the image of the ministry is obscured, diffuse, undramatic, purposeless. In the eyes of the coming generation the task of the minister is ill defined. Collegians . . . tend to view the minister as a competitive institutionalist, grabbing at whatever attention he can get in his community, concerned with budgetary needs, presenting a false front to the world and to other churches, ministering to the most traditional and defensive and uncreative element in the community.[14]

No wonder that the spontaneous worry of some men in college who choose the ministry is "how to tell their parents"! Our problem is this: *We have enough good men who are fit for the ministry, but we do not have a ministry that is fit for our best men.*

Many good laymen and ministers will protest this statement. They may have a different personal understanding of the pastoral ministry. Let us hope there are many who do. Certainly some ministers have transcended the distortions of the pastorate as we have described them. But for the majority of church members, it seems, the image projected by a majority of pastors is an unfortunate one. And, in this country, the majority rules.

Still, a remnant remains. One young minister of a small Pres-

[14] November 7, 1962, p. 1362.

byterian church in Vermont described his protest in a candidly frank article in *Pulpit* magazine. He, too, is concerned about the work of the ministry, and he deplores the stereotype to which a small-town pastor is expected to conform. He says that "the small-town minister is driven more and more into himself. . . . It is no wonder so many give up. They become assistants in large churches. They join special, inner-city projects. Possibly, with a perverse glee, they become board officials or religious journalists and join the ranks of the 'tormentors.' Or they give in to the universal expectations and become the kind of minister everybody seems to want." [15]

This man does not want to give in. He is convinced that the ministry is still a high calling, that it still must deal with real problems and be an opportunity for significant work in the name of Jesus Christ. He concludes that the "Christian community . . . ought to expend a bit more energy in making itself creatively useful and therefore more bearable." This man also says that if the pastoral ministry does not become more creatively useful, "the only honest advice to the thoughtful and serious young Christian would be: 'Whatever you do, do not be a minister. It is no job for a serious Christian.' "

Whatever you do, do not be a minister! It is no job for a serious Christian!!!

How many others have come to this shocking conclusion? A primary task of the church is to minister, whether it be through persons or groups of persons. If the contemporary nature of the pastoral ministry leads conscientious and sincere young men to conclude that there are better ways for serious Christians to serve, then the church must stop right now and take stock of

[15] Daniel C. Reuter, "A Young Minister's Dilemma," *The Pulpit*, July, 1961, pp. 26-28. Copyrighted by The Christian Century Foundation.

its ministry. Each denomination needs to do this in the light of its own theology and its own history.

It needs to be done for the sake of young men and women who want to serve God and their fellow man in the local church.

It needs to be done for the sake of the denomination itself. It needs to be done for the sake of the kingdom of God.

chapter 2

The Equipping Ministry

> *And these were his gifts: some to be*
> *apostles, some prophets, some evan-*
> *gelists, some pastors and teachers, to*
> *equip God's people for work in his*
> *service, to the building up of the body*
> *of Christ.*   EPH. 4:11-12 (N.E.B.)

IT IS CLEAR FROM THE NEW TESTAMENT THAT THE STANDARDS OF success for the Christian life are distinctly different from the standards of success which the American culture has set for itself in the twentieth century. Perhaps the outstanding examples of the church's adoption of these foreign criteria for itself are the obvious social separations that characterize Protestant churches. The apparent fact that most Protestant congregations are composed of well-dressed white people of middle-class communities is an indication that the churches have appropriated the standards of "the world" to measure their achievements. It is easy to see how old-line Protestant denominations have almost abandoned the central areas of American cities and have alienated themselves from those Americans

38

who don't happen to have white skins, white-collar jobs, and nice, white-stone houses in the suburbs.[1]

The retreat which the churches have made is comparable to that which its ministry has made as well. The growing area for Protestant denominations is in the suburbs, simply because new churches in these areas are quickly filled and easily financed by people who live in the upper social strata. It is, obviously, a matter of dollars and cents, symbols of the status which the church is seeking for itself. Yet the primary reason for the sickness of the church and its ministry today is this very search for status. It is the wrong goal for Christian groups, and wrong goals have a way of stimulating wrong means. Status is being sought, too, through the Protestant ministry, yet the nature of the gospel which ministers preach in whole or in part makes it virtually impossible for status really to be found. The concepts which undergird the Christian gospel and certainly the Christian ministry deal with ideas and beliefs which have nothing to do with status. They imply sacrifice, service, self-giving love, and concern for others. The New Testament repeats itself many times in this regard, as it tells us to take up our crosses and give comfort to the afflicted and afflict the comfortable. One can scarcely lose his life and still achieve status, and one can seldom *preach* the loss of life for Christ's cause in any seriousness and still *expect* to gain the plaudits of our society.

The religious status-seekers of the New Testament were the Pharisees, and Jesus condemned them for distorting their proper role. They were the most "religious" people of their day, and yet they weren't really religious because their religion had become professional. It had become a business. Christ's injunction against titles and the status ministry is very clear and direct in Matthew 23:

[1] See Gibson Winter, *The Suburban Captivity of the Churches* (New York: Doubleday, 1961), for a careful analysis of this retreat.

The doctors of the law and the Pharisees sit in the chair of Moses; therefore do what they tell you; pay attention to their words. But do not follow their practice; for they say one thing and do another. They make up heavy packs and pile them on men's shoulders, but will not raise a finger to lift the load themselves. Whatever they do is done for show. They go about with broad phylacteries and wear deep fringes on their robes; they like to have places of honour at feasts and the chief seats in synagogues, to be greeted respectfully in the street, and to be addressed as "rabbi".

But you must not be called "rabbi"; for you have one Rabbi, and you are all brothers. Do not call any man on earth "father"; for you have one Father, and he is in heaven. Nor must you be called "teacher"; you have one Teacher, the Messiah. The greatest among you must be your servant. For whoever exalts himself will be humbled; and whoever humbles himself will be exalted.

MATT. 23:2-12 (N.E.B.)

Surely what the work of the ministry should be patterned after would be more like the figure of Christ washing his disciples' feet than the Pharisee praying in the temple. Yet, in actual practice the roles which Protestant pastors are expected to play and usually do play are frequently patterned more nearly after the Pharisee than the servant. The crucial difference in the two kinds of ministry is this: One is a ministry built upon status; the other is concerned with function.

The functional ministry has no intrinsic honor or prestige. The role of servant implies service, not status. Its value and its main purpose rest in its ability to "serve," to "equip," to "encourage," and to "build up." A ministry of status, on the other hand, is more accurately described by a different vocabulary. A status-ministry "represents," "officiates," "pronounces," and "*is* built up." Elton Trueblood has indicated these differences in conception pointedly in these words:

40

[The functional ministry] has nothing to do with status or honor and [its] entire function is a loving, modest concern for the nourishment of the Divine Seed in each human heart. The good clergymen, in the established churches, undoubtedly perform this noble function, but part of their effectiveness is cancelled by the addition of factors of status. . . . To this day many clergymen are almost forced into a position of artificiality. They are expected to be the officially religious men, always praying at banquets, always giving the address of welcome and being accorded an ambiguous honor in return. Thousands of lay people refuse to call clergymen simply by their names, without some honorific title. When asked why this is, they reply that to fail to use a title would be lacking in respect. No doubt this is why Christ said His followers were not to use such titles. He saw the danger and warned almost fruitlessly against it.[2]

Of course, it will be impossible to have a ministry that is completely devoid of status features. Good men who serve other people are often honored in return out of appreciation and gratitude. We would be naïve if we said that an effective Christian ministry could have significant influence in American society and not have some prestige and be accorded some honors. For example, Albert Schweitzer is one who has great prestige and a status probably unmatched by any other religious leader of our time. Yet, Albert Schweitzer is an excellent illustration at the same time of the point which must be made: he has not sought fame or status or prestige; in fact, his greatness lies in the fact that he deserted the kind of honorific position which society offered and which many ministers actually seem to seek. The approval of men should not be "built in," and it should not be regarded by the ministry or the laymen as the pastor's due. The Protestant ministry possesses no keys of the kingdom either, no mysterious powers such as are accorded to the Roman

[2] D. Elton Trueblood, "The Paradox of the Quaker Ministry," 1960 Quaker Lecture of Indiana Yearly Meeting, p. 11.

clergy, from which he can derive ecclesiastical prestige and honor.

The New Testament emphasis on the functional or equipping ministry is no more clearly stated than in Eph. 4:11-12:

And these were his gifts: some to be apostles, some prophets, some evangelists, some pastors and teachers, to equip God's people for work in his service, to the building up of the body of Christ. (N.E.B.)

The New English Bible translates and punctuates this passage properly by clearly showing that the work of "pastors and teachers" is "to equip God's people for work in his service." This passage emphasizes, in other words, that God has given some men the special ability for and responsibility of being "pastors and teachers" and helping others to develop their own ministries. What we must make clear is this: it is always bad to make religion professional; it is not bad to make the pastor a professional. To be an equipping minister will require skill, knowledge, and great sensitivity. In this sense the minister ought to be a "professional," one who has a special ability in performing that kind of ministry which helps other people to perform their ministry, whatever it may be.

A ministry of status, on the contrary, seeks consciously or unconsciously to perpetuate itself. A functional ministry seeks to work itself out of a job, and theoretically the most successful pastor would be the man who has discovered, developed, trained, and nurtured the various ministries of a congregation to the point where he is no longer needed. The rewards which come to this kind of ministry are real ones, but they are not like the honorific recognition which comes to the status ministry. Satisfaction comes to the "equipping" minister as he sees develop, partly through his work, a *ministering church*, not a *minister-sponsoring* church. The individual witnesses of members in a congregation will, hopefully, be many, as will whole church efforts in missionary and service causes. Working constantly and working hard, but working behind the scenes, will be the minister as he seeks to equip his congregation for their tasks.

Robert Raines, who has developed and demonstrated the equipping ministry in his congregations, describes it in this way:

The clergyman's abiding frustration is that in doing the many things that are useful, he may be prevented from doing the one thing needful. It is being suggested here that the one thing needful in the role of the clergyman for our time is that he prepare his people for their ministry in the church and in the world. *The chief task of the clergyman is to equip his people for their ministry.* All his work is to this end. The functions of preacher, prophet, pastor, priest, evangelist, counselor, and administrator find their proper places in the equipping ministry. The purpose of this ministry is that the people shall be trained and outfitted for their work in the church and in the world.[3]

Again, the basic idea is that the minister is not to be *the* preacher, *the* pastor, *the* prophet, *the* priest, and *the* administrator FOR his church. Instead, his task is to equip members of his congregation so that they might become preachers, pastors, prophets, priests, and administrators themselves.

Raines uses the figure of a foreman in a plant as an analogy for the equipping ministry:

A layman said to me recently, "Your job is like that of a foreman in a plant. A foreman has a twofold responsibility. First he must teach and train his men to do their work. Second, he is responsible for their production. He must watch over them, guiding them and

[3] Raines, *op. cit.,* p. 141.

encouraging them to produce. So, you as a clergyman have to train us for our ministry, and then help us to fulfill our mission to produce. We are called to "go and bear fruit"; you are called to see that we do it.[4]

Not a symbol, not a representative, not one who is professionally good—the equipping ministry is marked by an emphasis on function, on the work of the Church rather than the prestige of the churches.

Akin to the emphasis upon an equipping ministry is the need for a certain understanding of the minister's financial situation. When the ministry is a matter of status rather than function, it is easy to think of a pastor as being "professionally good." He is paid enough to allow him to represent his congregation appropriately and to present the kind of appearance that the membership likes to see him make. However, when the image of the minister is built upon the idea of function, the understanding of his financial situation is changed. He is *set free* financially to do full time what his members can only do part-time. He is not paid for being a symbol; he is merely released from the burden of having to make a living so that he can concentrate on his main task. It is important that we remember that many of the earlier preachers and religious leaders of frontier America were men who were set free because of independent wealth—like Alexander Campbell—or worked just enough to provide for their basic needs—like John Woolman. In either case they were not paid for an office; they were liberated to perform their special ministries.

The idea of a man set free to equip others for their ministries is not a new concept. Indeed it is an old idea, and perhaps the most surprising thing about this understanding of the ministry is its seeming freshness and newness today. The

[4] *Ibid.*, p. 142.

44

idea of the equipping ministry is grounded in the New Testament, as we have seen, and also it is an idea that has been periodically discovered by concerned Christians over the centuries. It is helpful to remember that many of the reforming movements which led to the birth of some of our denominations had within them a criticism of clerical practices and the clerical image. The Reformation itself, as we all know, gave birth to one of the great ideas of Christianity—"the priesthood of all believers."

Implied in this idea are two concepts which are relevant to the image of the ministry. One, of course, is the emphasis on every Christian's ability and opportunity to worship God directly and personally. A special class of priests to whom man must confess is not necessary. The other concept goes even further, but it is taken far less seriously. Yet, for many of us the "priesthood of all believers" means that distinctions between laymen and ministers are erased. This idea is the great equalizer among Christians, because it made clear that the only separation which logically can exist among them is a separation in terms of talents and functions. The Reformation made the Bible available to all people, but it also did something else. It called attention to a fact which the early church took for granted: the call to be a Christian is in itself the call to be a minister.

The seventeenth-century Quakers were among those who grasped this implication most clearly. Once again we must remember that part of the Quaker understanding of the universal ministry of Christians was a reaction against a "status clergy." George Fox disparagingly referred to the clergy of his day as "hireling priests," primarily because so many clergymen of seventeenth-century England regarded their roles as ministers to be like professional jobs or a means of receiving special privileges and possibly even political advantage. Special titles and special honors were not due to the clergy, Fox held, simply because they were clergymen. Early Friends wanted to make very clear that the promotion of the gospel is *not* analagous to a secular profession.

At the same time, however, Friends believed in and, more important, amply demonstrated the reality of a *particular* as well as a *universal* ministry. The stereotype in most people's minds that the Friends did not have ministers is inaccurate. It is nearer the truth to say that they did not have laymen, and they did not have a status ministry. Robert Barclay, a contemporary of George Fox and the most systematic theologian among early Friends, was keenly aware of the universal *and* the particular ministries. In his *Apology* he writes:

We do believe and affirm that some are more particularly called to the work of the ministry, and therefore are fitted of the Lord for that purpose; whose work is more constantly and particularly to instruct, exhort, admonish, oversee, and watch over their brethren; and that . . . there is something more incumbent upon them in that respect than upon every common believer.[5]

The universal ministry does not just happen; it is the result of the particular ministry, of the work of those who have demonstrated special knowledge, special talents, and special interests. Those who are involved in the particular or equipping ministry are paid so that they will not go hungry and have clothes to wear and a place to live. They are set free for their tasks, but the ministry is not a place for men financially to do "as well as they can." They are not paid because they are good; they are paid so that they won't have to spend their time

[5] Book X, article 26.

working at a certain job but can be busy building up the universal ministry.

It is not surprising to discover, also, that the Disciples of Christ, the largest indigenous denomination in this country, began with an understanding of the ministry very much like that of the Quakers. Alexander Campbell, from the outset of his ministry, refused to accept any money for his preaching, a fact which was made possible by the gift of a farm to him by his well-to-do father-in-law. Interestingly enough, this situation is comparable to that of Robert Barclay who inherited an estate from his father, Colonel David Barclay, and who likewise was released for his religious labors. They did not have to make a living as ministers, in other words, so they were freed from the temptation of using the ministry for financial success. This situation made it possible for them to focus upon their real tasks, and both Campbell and Barclay saw the need for a responsible ministry to encourage the universal ministry.

Like George Fox who preceded him, Campbell's reforming movement was partly an objection to the status ministry of his time. In Garrison and DeGroot's history of the Disciples, Campbell's disapproval of the Protestant ministry of his day is clear:

[In Campbell's opinion] the clergy had elaborated simple Christianity with so much ecclesiastical machinery and theological lore that they had made themselves indispensable for administering the one and understanding the other. They had made it so complicated that only experts could handle it—and they were the experts. All the innovations and intricacies by which the churches were divided were the inventions of the clergy. So there had come into existence a Protestant priesthood which stood between the people and the Bible. These "hireling priests" were pilloried . . . as proud, pretentious, covetous, shrewd in advancing their personal and sectarian interests, addicted to affectations of piety and professional mannerisms of speech and dress, loving to be addressed by such titles as "Reverend,"

47

by professing to have had a divine "call" to the ministry which made their exalted position impregnable.[6]

Campbell's movement, like Fox's, was an effort to return to New Testament Christianity. His objections to the clergy were not just personal objections but based upon the belief that the "status ministry" was not grounded in the New Testament. Campbell and Fox had discovered what we must rediscover today: a reform within a church invariably demands a reform among its leaders. Whenever the church deserts its original dependence upon the universal ministry, it finds itself nurturing a ministry of status and title.

The status ministry is a denial of the Protestant concept of the priesthood of all believers. Much of our trouble today is simply the result of this denial. Our contemporary rejection of it has not been a conscious matter, and it has not been the deliberate attempt of Protestant ministers who have sought special honors. No, as in the past, it has simply "happened." It has happened because Christian people are continually tempted to delegate their religious and ethical responsibilities to someone else "more qualified." There is, after all, an immense feeling of relief that comes from knowing some other person is responsible. Prayer becomes something that can only be done—at least publicly—when one commands a special theological vocabulary. Ministry is a matter of officiating at certain ceremonies, and the unofficial Christian assumes that he cannot act in an official capacity. Ministers come to agree with this point of view, too, and doubtless some even delight in it. So, it "happens," and one day Christians discover that the role of their ministers is more completely dominated by protocol than by the dictates of function.

[6] Garrison and DeGroot, *The Disciples of Christ, A History* (St. Louis: Bethany Press, 1948), pp. 176 ff.

When the status ministry is dominant, as it is now, the whole church suffers. Religion becomes the concern of the professional few, and those few either perpetuate the image or are forced into the position of constantly trying to do their real work while struggling against it. One ex-pastor stated his revulsion to this dilemma in these words:

I am especially uneasy over the self-image I have found in a number of younger pastors. Frequently they pattern themselves after some "successful" Protestant ministers who gather to themselves professional mannerisms and accouterments which unmistakably set themselves apart from the other members, however faithful they may be. With the use of the title "reverend," a clergy sign on their cars, a lapel cross, a well-worn New Testament (soft-backed preferred) in hand, the formal dark blue or black suit and hat, usually goes the assumption, "I am a minister; therefore, I am different from you. Don't forget the 10% clergy discount, please."

The primary objection this man makes is to what he regards as the false separation between Christians on the basis of status symbols. Certainly he has a point, for such an image as he describes will not give us the proper guidance for the equipping ministry. Ministers who adopt for themselves such standards of success will not save us; they will merely contribute to our problem.

The need to recapture the New Testament and Reformation insights about the ministry is not the only reason why a new image of the Protestant ministry must evolve. The other reason, equally important, is simply that the contemporary situation in the local church is desperate. In terms of real sacrifice, real service, and real ministry by the local congregation, very few instances of vital Christianity can be found. Numerous observers of the religious scene have noted the great shallowness and weakness of the Christian faith in the churches. Bishop

Pike undoubtedly disturbed many in a recent Christmas message which was published in a national magazine. Entitled "Christianity Is in Retreat," the article was highly controversial, but it noted several of the most serious deficiences of the church today. He pointed out that there is much superficial evidence of progress such as increased church membership, the high sale of religious books, and many church building programs; but Bishop Pike made abundantly clear that "without question the opportunities for a meaningful, ministering church are greater than ever before. . . . But the condition of our society is proof that the opportunities have not been seized." [7]

Here, briefly stated, is why a new, equipping ministry must be shaped. We need churches that judge themselves by the standards of the New Testament, and ministers who do the same. It is true that many in the church do not want a functional ministry, but it is also painfully apparent that many who are failing to find reason and purpose in their lives through the church want something better than they are now getting. The church will become something better if its ministry gives it new guidance, new understanding, and certainly a better example than it now is giving. The churches need religious leadership, but the real problem is how to provide the leadership and still have people assume responsibility for their own ministry.

The equipping ministry tries to do both things; it seeks to define its own image in terms of its task of developing the lay ministry. It is our best hope for revitalizing a stagnant church without causing Christians to become overly dependent upon itself. The present Protestant ministry is unsatisfactory because it is preoccupied with status rather than function and because it is too easily dominated and informed by the standards of

[7] *Look,* December 20, 1960, p. 24.

American society. A new, equipping ministry must be stronger than the churches it serves, attractive to young Christians who are searching for tangible ways of serving God, and challenging enough to demand the very best minds and hearts which are available. It is presumptuous to assume that one or two of us can define such a ministry, but it is a far greater error not to try.

chapter 3

The Builder of Community

Where the Fellowship is lacking the
Church invisible is lacking and the
Kingdom of God has not yet come.
—THOMAS KELLY

THERE ARE MANY FIGURES OF SPEECH USED TO DESCRIBE THE
Church of Jesus Christ. It is called the "body of Christ," "the
living Fellowship," or the "redemptive community." Another
word which has been popular in theological conversation in
recent years is *koinonia,* the Greek word in the New Testament usually translated by "fellowship," which implies a very
deep degree of closeness and mutual concern. All these words,
however, are efforts to describe what the church ought to be,
or ought to become, or is in its ideal state. It ought to be a
living fellowship; it ought to be *koinonia.*

Unfortunately, while there is general agreement as to what
ought to be the case, most ministers and most church leaders
do not seem to be working very hard to achieve Christian community. Instead, their efforts go into building audiences,
elaborate organizations, and a schedule of church related ac-

tivities. There is general agreement as to our goal, but there is very little practice in making the hope become a reality.

In fact, the point at which the modern church has retreated the most, at least on the local level, is in its loss of "community." The idea, indeed the reality, of the gathered community in the New Testament as a central part of the Christian effort is obvious. Nearly all the New Testament letters were addressed to such gathered communities or redemptive fellowships. These groups of Christians were synonymous with the church. We must never forget either that the New Testament itself is the product of the gathered church, rather than the gathered church being the product of the New Testament.

Throughout history, too, most religious movements and sects that have come into existence have demonstrated in their earliest stages genuine *koinonia*. Like the New Testament Christians, they have had to do so. They have had to exhibit real Christian love and concern of members for each other to be able to survive persecution and attack. To a great extent these groups have been both religious and economic units, as the members have found themselves dependent upon one another for material support. These fellowship groups have been, in actuality, something like large families, with common participation and sharing by the group in the important events and crises of life—such as birth, marriage, death, suffering, and physical need.

Once the rural church in America demonstrated this kind of concern for the material and spiritual needs of its members. The image of the rural church ethic pictures members and neighbors going together to raise a new barn after a burning or to share chores in times of crises. This image includes the country church and the neat cemetery behind it too, as the reality of death was more closely associated with the church then than now. We recall, also, the fact that the rural church was the social center of the community and these factors made it more easily possible for the local, rural church to be something like a loving community of persons who truly cared for one another. To some extent this is an idyllic picture produced partly by nostalgic elders. Yet it was also frequently realized.

Today, America is no longer rural. Our society is highly mobile, and this very mobility makes it difficult for ties of love and concern to bind persons together. It is simply difficult for redemptive communities to be built due to a lack of time and stability. In our bureaucratic, welfare-minded society, furthermore, many of the personal needs which the local church sought to meet out of Christian love and compassion are now handled by governmental agencies. Social security, health insurance, life insurance, welfare boards, and many other agencies have taken over some of the functions formerly handled by the church. Then, too, the church is under no real threat of persecution in this country, and the witness of history clearly shows that persecution is a unifying and adhesive force in the building of Christian community.

These facts indicate why it is hard to have *koinonia* in the local church today. Many sociological forces are working against it. Yet, *koinonia* is the missing element in most churches. How many of our main-line Protestant congregations could be said to be like a family today? Most could be said to be more like gatherings of acquaintances who may vaguely recognize one another when sighted across the room at worship on certain Sunday mornings.

It is true, of course, that every church in every denomination has its hard core. However, many times this hard core demonstrates loyalty and concern toward a different object than is the case in real *koinonia*. Too often its loyalty and devotion are not directed toward persons who are members of a community but toward the structure and organization of the church-institution. Hard-core members are concerned that old First Church have a dignified and respected pastor. They see to it that the sanctuary is redecorated regularly, and they make sure that the reputation of their beloved institution passes through the years without blemish or debt.

But this is not "community" in the Christian sense. It is not *koinonia*. It is not a demonstration of a loving fellowship. Members of most churches feel loyalty toward some other members because they are personal friends or fellow Rotarians or bridge partners. They practice brotherly love toward some because they like them anyhow. However, it is not usually characteristic of even the hard-core members of most Protestant churches to be deeply concerned about others just because they are members of the same church and followers of the same Christ.

Of course, some churches have not failed so miserably to be living fellowships as others. Lest these few groups now pause to congratulate themselves, however, it must be made clear that there is often a reason for this that cannot be distinctly traced to the special blessing of the Holy Spirit. Such churches are usually small, even though they don't want to be small, and smallness makes the achievement of community more nearly possible. The sense of community and mutual concern that exists in some places, in other words, is almost an accident. It is certainly not typical. Nevertheless, *koinonia* is something that must be found or rediscovered or developed. If Christians, to some degree, have it or its vestiges, it should not be taken lightly nor cast aside in an effort to be numerically successful.

This fact must be one of the distinctive shaping ingredients of the work of the Protestant pastor. The Christian Church should be a redemptive community, but it often is not. Pastors should be builders of Christian community, but most of them are not. One of his functions—perhaps the primary one—is to be a builder of a "living fellowship" rather than a builder of prestige, of buildings, or of an institution. It is relatively easy to make a success story out of a local church. It is extremely difficult to build a community of persons.

It must be understood, of course, that a pastor by himself cannot build community. However, it is also a matter of fact that he can do a lot to set the conditions out of which *koinonia* can grow. If the pastor conceives of his task as getting all sizes and shapes of people out to public meetings, he risks the opportunity for real fellowship. Such efforts, even when successful, usually produce nice fat totals for the yearly reports, but they also produce a congregation of individuals who are listeners and strangers. The point we seek to make is this: If a pastor sees as his task the building and nurturing of a "community" rather than an "audience" of persons, the programs he sponsors and the preaching he does and the way he spends his time will be distinctly affected.

Among the expectations which his congregation has for him, the pastor can best take advantage of his role as organizer or administrator. He will be expected, and this is a reasonable expectation, to give guidance as to what is important for Christians to do and how they should go about it. For example, one of the best ways to breed a congregation of strangers is to have simple, quick, and easy requirements for membership. It may be that a man can enter the door at 10:30 on a Sunday morning a non-church member and leave at 11:30 an accredited and official part of the membership list, but this act will not make him a member of the Christian community. There should be a lengthy waiting period. The prospective member should be encouraged to learn the meaning of community; he ought to have the opportunity to know the people with whom he is to be joined, and others in the church ought to have time to show that they want to welcome and receive him in more than a superficial and

56

trivial way. In ways like these community can be developed.

The Protestant pastor should take advantage of his administrative role in order to set the conditions out of which real fellowship emerges. His job is to bless the tie that binds, not bless the tides that bring crowds of strangers together. Some programs, meetings, and gatherings promote community; others do not. Recently a woman wrote a letter to "Dear Abby" which illustrates almost perfectly the kind of activities the Protestant pastor should not bless. Her letter is quoted in part:

Dear Abby:

My husband and I are very active in our church, but my husband is overdoing it. He attends board meetings, men's club meetings, he is on the planning committee for all fund-raising affairs, and he never misses a bingo game, carnival or square dance. . . . I could cope with "another woman," but how does a wife compete with God?

Abby's answer included this statement which speaks to our condition:

Dear Church widow:

Do not confuse God with bingo, square dances and carnivals. Granted, most churches need funds (and fund-raising affairs) for survival, but I think your husband is more interested in "fun-raising." Do a little roof-raising.[1]

Her point is well taken. Protestant pastors have confused activities with God's business. It is time that we did a little roof-raising with the way we encourage Christian people to spend their time and energy in the name of God. Meetings should be held, but they should be meetings with a redemptive purpose.

The building of community often meets opposition. There

[1] "Dear Abby," July 31, 1961. Used by permission.

is a school of thought that promotes the idea that the good church is the active church that is "doing things." Those who adhere to this theory admire Bible-reading marathons which start at 3:00 A.M. and end twenty-four hours later. We should not be surprised to learn that they favor three meetings for men, women, and young people of the church—to be held simultaneously, of course—on the topic: "Why don't families spend more time together?"

Surely this is one of the reasons why so few churches are in any real sense Christian communities today. As their members look over their schedules of church committees, meetings, fellowship groups, rummage sales, and planning sessions, it is no wonder so many have concluded that Christianity is only helpful to people with hyperactive thyroids. As wives go out one door to one meeting, husbands another door to another meeting, and the children start screaming at the sight of another baby-sitter, most normal Christians probably want to stop and cry: "Don't just do something, stand there!" The minister should sponsor and stimulate only those meetings and programs which aid, not hinder, the development of community.

It is rather easy to state what a pastor should *not* encourage if he is to be preoccupied with building community. A good general rule to follow is this: Activities should be eliminated or reduced in number which perpetually (1) inspire dissension, bad feelings, and arguments; (2) wear people out physically and mentally to such a degree that they vow never to get involved again; and (3) cause people to wonder *why* they are doing what they are doing. If activities judged by these standards be eliminated, church buildings would gather dust considerably faster than they do now. Indeed, the major difference between people who are part of a community and those who are part of an audience can be judged by these same standards. (1) In a fellowship of persons dissension and bad feelings can usually be faced and overcome. Certainly they are not continually inspired. (2) Getting worn out is not in itself bad, but getting worn out for a trivial reason is. (3) Members of real fellowships are usually able to justify the existence of their own group, or, in this case, their church activities in good conscience.

In stating exactly what a pastor should do as a builder of community, one runs the risk of being too specific. What works in one situation may not work in another. It is also true that the existence of real Christian community in the long run seems to depend on the activity of the Holy Spirit, and not our best laid plans, because our efforts to guarantee its existence have backfired too often for any of us to feel very much confidence about our pet solutions.

However, those who have been wrestling with the problem of how to build community in the local church have found certain ideas more effective than others. In terms of goals, in terms of what pastors want to achieve, these ideas offer examples, at least, of what is meant by building community instead of bubbling with activity. The minister should want to build a church which, as Howard Brinton says, "is like a large family whose members are dependent on one another . . . for spiritual well-being." [2]

One way to do this is through the encouragement and the development of small fellowship or study groups. This idea, of course, while relatively new, is becoming increasingly well-known. All over the country churches have within themselves small groups meeting regularly for study, prayer, self-understanding, or discussion. Undoubtedly, some of these groups fail to help build community because man has the clever ability to transform almost any significant effort into trivial activity. Nevertheless, there is almost consistent testimony that in these

[2] Howard Brinton, *Friends for 300 Years* (New York: Harper & Row, 1952), p. 126.

groups something important has been happening. Two recent books, in fact, emphatically say that the development of small groups is essential to the nurturing of a spirit of love within a congregation. What is significant about these books, furthermore, is the fact that both are primarily descriptions of what is happening in churches where the small group approach has been used. Robert Raines states in *New Life in the Church* that "the small group is a medium through which God has evidently chosen to work in powerful and permanent ways to help people start growing and continue to grow in Christ." [3] It is the "strategy" for new life in our churches. G. Don Gilmore is equally enthusiastic for small groups in his moving description of how a church became a fellowship of persons.[4] He credits the Yokefellow movement with its small-group, common discipline formula with being "the instrument of a genuine spiritual revival across our church." Even with their deficiencies, it is true that within the small fellowship group persons do get to know one another better; they are able to discover mutual weaknesses, and frequently they are able to face common problems. Closeness becomes more possible. Members have fewer restrictions on their efforts to relate the Christian faith as they understand it to their real problems of daily living.

Retreats, too, help build community. There is something about getting off in the woods with the explicit intention of growing in faith and understanding that draws people out of themselves and closer together. Once again retreats are nothing new, yet most church members undoubtedly think that a retreat is either a military term meaning the opposite of advance, or a damp house where monks eat unleavened bread.

Another way in which the pastor helps build community is

[3] Raines, *op. cit.*, p. 79.

[4] G. Don Gilmore, *In the Midst* (Grand Rapids: Eerdmans Pub. Co., 1962), p. 44.

through the use and guidance of natural groups within the church. A few years ago Wesley Shrader wrote an article in *Life* magazine which was entitled, "The Most Wasted Hour of the Week." The hour of which he wrote was the Sunday-school period on Sunday morning, and the tremendous volume of mail the magazine received was an indication that he either made a point or stepped on some toes. What we need to see is that there are undoubtedly Sunday-school classes which are wasting their hours but which could be transformed into fellowship groups.

For example, an adult class in one church has over the years probably been severely lacking in terms of educational content. This is highly unfortunate, and yet this same group enjoys very close relationships within itself and this helps to justify its existence. Should a member die, all other members gather to share in a worship service in his honor. Recently, when one member was critically ill, several members of the group performed services of real help and concern for his family. This was made more significant because the critically ill person was an active politician, and several of those who were so deeply concerned were equally passionate about the political stand of the opposition party. For religious loyalties to transcend political loyalties in our day is, unfortunately, unusual. Several years ago, too, this class set up a scholarship for the son of one of their members who died suddenly and tragically. Indeed, the problem that this class faces is the temptation to be cliquish, but there is little doubt that the expressions of love and concern of one member for another are genuine.

The pastor by himself, we repeat, cannot create such a spirit of community. But he can encourage it. He can recognize it when it happens. He can point to it as an example. He can lay before those classes wasting their hours the challenge of becoming a community of Christian persons.

In the program which the pastor encourages, he must remember that real Christian fellowship is usually a by-product, and those meetings which are planned with the explicit intention of producing "jolly good fellowship" usually fail. The kind of Christian *koinonia* the pastor hopes to see emerge within a congregation will be produced most frequently when people have the opportunity to share a common experience that is both *deep* and *important*. Antoine de Saint Exupéry in *Wind, Sand and Stars* has described the best philosophy for achieving a sense of community: "Life has taught us that love does not consist in gazing at each other but in looking outward together in the same direction. There is no comradeship except through union in the same high effort." [5]

Christian *koinonia* will not be achieved merely by going on record as being for it; nor can it be forced; nor—usually—does it happen through the trivial efforts of preparing a bean supper which has as its purpose the buying of new plastic curtains for the church kitchen. In fact, the reason why most money-raising efforts do not produce Christian community is because too few members share the same affection for the cause someone else has said *ought* to be theirs.

Frank Laubach once said in a public address: "You have to go out, see the world, and have your heart broken. Then you can help." The pastor's task as a builder of community includes providing in the local church those occasions through which people can see more of the world around them, "have their hearts broken," and then be united in "the same high effort." There is no substitute, in other words, for work and experience. Work projects in which compassion is the obvious reason for the work belong, therefore, in the church program of high-school and college young people. For example, weekend work camps offer one of the best ways for youth to have the chance

[5] (New York: Reynal & Hitchcock, 1939), p. 288.

to experience Christian fellowship. Nearly every denomination sponsors such opportunities for high-school and college students, and many others would become available if more pastors encouraged their use.

A significant demonstration of this principle in action was observed at Earlham College several years ago when students and faculty co-operated closely over a period of several weeks in the actual construction of the college meeting house. This was a major project, and not only was the end result physically beautiful and functional, but the general spirit of affection and fellowship which was produced was so real that it lasted as long as the participating students remained on campus.

Christian fellowship will be the by-product of the *work* of men, women, and young people in our churches—if they can experience the reason for the work. Work in race relations takes on reality if people hear and see the problems Negroes face as second-class citizens. One group learned this merely by conducting a series of interviews with Negroes and whites in an integrated neighborhood. The knowledge of what segregation in housing was really like was grasped in a far more effective way than could ever be communicated through sermons, group discussions, or lectures. Another Presbyterian church sponsored monthly canteens and programs for groups at a nearby mental hospital. The experience they had was typical: the patients were pleased and the workers were welded into a real fellowship. When the pastor encourages and shares in a program of actual work which has a redemptive purpose, community is built and the kingdom of God is served.

Again, the pastor can allow many members of his congregation to share in the redemptive activities for which he, in most situations, is expected to be individually responsible. It is not a sign of a redemptive fellowship when a pastor regularly and faithfully calls on the sick, the shut-in, and the aged. This merely indicates that a church has hired a minister who, because he wants to or because he is paid to, visits such persons. The programs the pastor promotes should be programs in which other members of the congregation visit the sick, the aged, and the shut-in.

Furthermore, the pastor should get more persons involved in the crucial matters of life with which the church has some connection but which are usually assumed to be only the pastor's responsibility. For example, should some members from a modern church call on a couple contemplating marriage to wish them well or possibly even to counsel with them, there is little doubt but that the couple would be more clearly aware of the general concern of their church for their forthcoming marriage. This kind of concern has been delegated to the pastor in most Protestant churches, yet it is a contradiction in terms to "delegate" concern. It can't be done. It is something like appointing a committee to worship God; it is something that cannot be carried out by a proxy. The matters of life, death, and crisis are matters with which the whole church should deal, and when it does it has come a long way towards being a redemptive community.

The idea of getting members to share in the redemptive work of a congregation is potentially a great one. A living example as to why this idea is so important to the life of the church has been given us in the work of Alcoholics Anonymous. The reason why AA "works" is because the alcoholic knows that the men and women trying to help him have been through what he has been through. He knows they understand. It is practically impossible, however, for the pastor—regardless of how sensitive and how concerned he wants to be—actually to share in many of the deep problems which church members have. He can have varying degrees of rapport with many, it is true, but if he has

64

been building a community of persons, the kind of help he is expected to give can be deepened and certainly multiplied.

Albert Schweitzer has given us a key to this method of multiplication in one of his early books:

The Fellowship of those who bear the Mark of Pain. Who are the members of this Fellowship? Those who have learnt by experience what physical pain and bodily anguish mean, belong together all the world over; they are united by a secret bond. One and all they know the horrors of suffering to which man can be exposed, and one and all they know the longing to be free from pain. He who has been delivered from pain must not think he is now free again, and at liberty to take life up just as it was before, entirely forgetful of the past. He is now a "man whose eyes are open" with regard to pain and anguish, and he must help to overcome those two enemies (so far as human power can control them) and to bring to others the deliverance which he has himself enjoyed.[6]

Stated in another way but conveying essentially the same truth, is the famous statement engraved on a bench near the Cornell University library:

> To those who shall sit here rejoicing,
> To those who shall sit here mourning,
> Sympathy and Greeting;
> So have we done in our time.

The minister, through general conversation and through particular contacts with individuals, can nurture the love-in-action of the church he serves by seeking out and using those who are in "the fellowship of those who bear the Mark of Pain." When

[6] Albert Schweitzer, *On the Edge of the Primeval Forest* (New York: The Macmillan Co., 1948), p. 116.

men share in the crises of their lives, a bond of love is built which is not easily broken.

One woman who lost her first child now sees as her special responsibility that of visiting and sharing the grief of other young mothers and fathers who "are sitting where once she sat." Frequently she writes a note or sees them briefly, but the scope of this ministry cannot be outlined and neither can the bond of love and understanding that is felt be described. The woman comes in the name of Christ; this is usually only implied but it is clearly understood. And this understanding helps build in two lives, the spirit of *koinonia*.

The same principle could be demonstrated in the case of persons who discover they have a retarded or subnormal child. In one instance a conscientious family attempted to keep a mentally retarded child at home with their other children because of a confused sense of duty, and this course of action resulted in some real harm to one of the normal children. Only when another woman who had experienced a similar tragedy in her own life shared with the mother the benefits of her struggle was she able to allow herself to place the child in an appropriate institution.

Indeed, the application of this principle to the pastoral situation is limitless. As broken marriages continue to be commonplace, the help that a divorcee (who is a concerned Christian) can give to others experiencing the heartbreak and stress of divorce is immeasurable. The same is true of the personal help that comes when a pastor guides church members into developing a relationship with some of the miserable young people who are forced, by pregnancy or the fear of it, into an early marriage. Some have survived this kind of bad beginning, and no one else in the world is quite so familiar with the intricate problems of such a situation as those who have struggled through it. The possibilities of this kind of multiplied ministry are enormous. Theoretically, at least, persons within a church could both consciously and unconsciously function as "fellow-sufferers"—as members of anonymous but real fellowships who are willing to share the memory of their crisis with another who feels sure he suffers alone.

We must be careful not to overdramatize these efforts, of course, although we have seen the principle applied in so many incidental and individual cases that there is little doubt but that a *program* along these lines could be encouraged in a local church. The place of a pastor, obviously, will have to be informal and his success in stimulating such efforts will depend in large measure upon how well and how intimately he knows the people whom he serves (an important argument for long pastorates and extensive personal contacts with members).

My wife and I have experienced, in a small way, the validity of the idea that pain unites persons and offers a means of spiritual communication more powerful than words could ever express. When we learned that our small daughter faced an eye operation, as young parents we were very anxious for her, even though the operation, the physician assured us, was "routine." (As if an operation is ever "routine" for those who care!) Yet, when some others whose children had undergone the same operation told us what to expect and communicated to us that they truly understood our anxiety, the hard moments became bearable. This is a small illustration of a large truth; real Christian fellowship is as deep as the experiences which promote it.

Because he is the one person who is aware of the needs of a congregation better than any other, the pastor can nurture *koinonia* by being continually alert to the opportunities for such redemptive activities. Upon learning of an individual who is to have major surgery, he can have a twofold response. He can visit the person himself, and he can drop the news to the "right" person whose history and experiences will allow him or her to perform a helpful ministry of personal sharing. In this way he builds a community of persons which is more like a large family than might have been thought possible in our cold, impersonal, overly busy world.

The development of small groups, the scheduling and planning of retreats, the transformation of Sunday-school classes, and the sharing of the redemptive ministry of concern are merely illustrations of what is meant by the pastor's responsibility to be a builder of community. Undoubtedly, there are many more ways of doing this, and undoubtedly, too, little communities exist within many churches already. However, what has been accidental should become intentional. A minister cannot control its happening, but he can control circumstances in which it can happen.

There is no question that there is real need for this kind of living fellowship in every Christian church in the land today. In fact, upon the premise of *koinonia,* most of the rest of the business with which a pastor should be concerned is built. Many of the problems which frustrate the minister exist because the church is not a community nor is there a major group which in some sense constitutes a living fellowship. The kind of life change which is usually called redemption can best take place in the midst of a gathering of loving, concerned people. Certainly, the life change can best be nurtured through the sustaining and understanding efforts of Christian people. A major end of the programs which the pastor places before his church for their adoption and approval should be the kind that allows redemption to take place.

The building of community is essential to the task of a pastor because it sets a context for the proclamation of the gospel. The gospel as it has been proclaimed over the years has included some rather touchy and controversial points. It has included such matters as pacifism, equality of the sexes and races, loving our unlovable neighbors, and our confounded enemies. Because of freedom of thought on some of these controversial matters, the consciences of good Christians have put them on opposite sides of issues and encouraged passionate feelings. The Protestant pastor, often having stronger feelings about some of these matters than most Christians and giving such issues greater study than many, sometimes finds himself at odds with his church. He may become a harmonizer who glosses over real differences, or a mere figurehead, and thereby survive, but he may also attempt to be loyal to his convictions and thereby run the risk of alienating his congregation. It is possible, too, that the pastor who finds himself in the distinct minority on these questions may proceed to demonstrate either the arrogance of self-appointed prophetism or the false humility of self-conscious martyrdom.

Yet, the essence of *koinonia* is that controversy breeds growth rather than dissension. When the pastor builds and becomes a part of a living fellowship, then the tough questions can be answered. In a truly concerned and living fellowship, the pastor becomes less and less an outsider. The people with whom he deals become people who themselves face certain pressures, who have been influenced by certain ideas, and who don't want radically different ideas from their own forced down their throats any more than the pastor does. In community both the pastor and his fellow Christians have their arrogance tempered by love and mutual respect.

In the atmosphere of a community, furthermore, the pastor has a good opportunity to avoid another serious liability of the Protestant ministry, namely, irresponsible moralism. Pastors are inclined to make judgments about many things; indeed, they should do so. However, such judgments—such moralisms, as it were—become irresponsible when the preacher is safely removed from having to share the consequences of the action he so eagerly prescribes. Lloyd Averill has provided us with an excellent illustration of this tendency. A minister was preaching eloquently and piously one day on the need for young people to give their lives to the foreign mission field. As he invited any so moved to come forward, he was thunderstruck to discover his own daughter among them, and he could not suppress the protest: "My God, I didn't mean you!" [7]

Ministers must be very careful to avoid that which pastors are so often accused of doing—talking about things which are the "other guy's" problem. There is a temptation to tell the factory worker he should not come home from work and merely collapse in a chair every night in front of his television set, but instead should read a good book or come to a church meeting. However, the pastor must be sensitive to the routine and pressures of that factory worker so that he understands the worker's attitude to such an extent that his criticisms will be fair. In turn, the factory worker will have to accept the pastor as an understanding and sensitive person before his criticisms will be heard. Such a relationship presupposes Christian community; it depends upon it.

Lloyd Averill makes this point clearly:

For too many ministers, the pulpit and pastoral functions are privileged sanctuaries which are not subject to the corrective and creative influences of the whole fellowship. Yet it is clear that this kind of isolation leads directly to preaching which is marked by professional goodness and irresponsible moralism. And it is equally clear that the only way to bridge our separation—to keep goodness from becoming professional and morality from becoming irresponsible—is to take our places humbly in the fellowship of those who

[7] "Lest I Be Disqualified," *The Pulpit,* July, 1961, p. 9. Copyrighted by The Christian Century Foundation.

forsake self-sufficiency and confess their common needs. . . . It is [in the church] that we must learn to bear one another's burdens in very concrete ways, sharing willingly, joyfully, and responsibly the full consequences of the fearful moral decisions which each is called to make.[8]

The reality of Christian community is a big step toward avoiding professionalism and separateness among the clergy. Only when a pastor builds a community by being part of it will he be able to avoid these errors.

Only in the context of community will constructive action take place. Christians in the twentieth century have had the inclination to make tolerance *the* virtue which must be preserved at all costs. Unfortunately, easy tolerance is usually based on the assumption that all values are equal or relative. Easy tolerance, in other words, often leads to easy action or no action at all. Or, at the other extreme, the concerned Christian has felt inhibited and unable to act on the dictates of his conscience because his point of view was so distinctly a minority one.

When people consider plans, ideas, and problems together in a serious and deep way, and when they understand and care for each other, it is more nearly possible to avoid cheap tolerance and frustrated consciences. The person who glibly declares that he thinks those who like to take Freedom Rides are entitled to do as they please, although such action is not his cup of tea, may be using his tolerance as an escape clause with his conscience. One must do more than merely be tolerant of, say, Freedom Riders, although unwilling to be one himself. In the context of a community the individual has an opportunity to say what he *will* do himself, not just what he will tolerate someone else's doing.

Again, the concerned Christian who finds himself frustrated

[8] *Ibid.*

because his convictions do not often find expression can be free in a community to a degree far greater than in the church where strangers gather to observe worship. When people come to love and appreciate each other even though they disagree, the person who stands with the minority feels more free to act at least in his own name if not in the name of his church. For example, Freedom Riders, pacifists, those opposed to capital punishment, those who plead for tolerance of Catholics and Jews, those who favor feeding the Red Chinese, those who advocate disarmament, and others find themselves accused by "outsiders" as Communists or dupes. In a community of persons, however, this seldom happens. One's opinion may be regarded as unwise or unrealistic, but the person himself is usually regarded as Christian and often receives a kind of grudging respect for his stand. At least the majority can have this feeling: "I don't like your ideas, but I trust you. God bless you in your efforts, and may he bless me in mine."

Finally, when there is a strong sense of living fellowship in the church, the congregation takes better advantage of its opportunities for outright service and concrete humanitarian or spiritual action. A cartoon once showed a picture of a woman lying in her sick bed, obviously in misery. In the sink were stacked piles of dirty dishes. A huge basket of clothes to be ironed sat nearby. Two dirty children were fighting in one corner, and in the other sat a cat which was licking milk from a bottle that had been broken. A smiling woman stood in the doorway, and the caption under the cartoon pictured her as saying: "Well, Florence, if there is anything I can do to help, don't hesitate to let me know."

When members of a congregation are out of touch with each other and their needs, they, too, see nothing they can do. True, the government and the insurance companies can provide for many of the needs for which the church once felt responsible. However, there are ways that the local church can help its members which are not taken advantage of, and certainly an impersonal agency like the government can scarcely indicate that it really cares for an individual. When the adults of a church are concerned about the welfare of its youth, it can help provide for their education through scholarships and through close association with its church-related schools. If only the pastor responds at the time of personal tragedy, the church has bypassed an opportunity to demonstrate *koinonia*. Family support, help for the mentally ill and their families, and guidance from many within the church for those who need it are fruits that come out of Christian communities which are bound together by more than a roof over the heads of a few people a few times a year.

It is central to the minister's task that he build community. The perfect Christian community, of course, does not exist. However, it is a goal which can never let the minister rest. Community building is a hard task. It may even be that there are some places which have so distorted the image of what a church should be that it is virtually impossible for any minister to help build such a fellowship of persons.

It is deeply disturbing to realize that this may be the case, yet building community is the proper business of the Protestant pastor. In doing his job he will probably find himself in the background, and for this reason this aspect of the work of the Protestant pastor will not be attractive to those who seek some kind of personal prestige or material success in the church. Yet, if dedicated young men seek truly to be servants of the living God, then building communities of Christian people is first on the list of what they must be doing.

Indeed, someone must be about this task, or our situation will become more—not less—desperate than it now is.

chapter 4

The Catalytic Agent

> *Good, honest, mechanic men and*
> *others, being possessed with a false*
> *opinion that it is not lawful for them*
> *to meddle with the ministry, do there-*
> *by neglect the gift in themselves.*
> —ROBERT BARCLAY

A DISTINGUISHED AND DEDICATED CHRISTIAN LAYMAN TELLS THIS
story:

I once asked a successful preacher what he would reply to forty
or fifty men who might come up to him at the close of some Sunday
service and say, "We feel we must do something about that sermon
of yours; what would you suggest?" He said, "Goodwin, I don't
know, we already have sixty ushers." [1]

Here is a good example of the situation existing in many
Protestant churches today. The pastor, it seems, thinks of his
local organization as having a very small "o" and his church as
having a very small "c." When he thinks in terms of what people

[1] W. H. Goodwin, "Delivering the Goods," *Laymen Speaking* (ed. by Wallace
Speers) (New York: Association Press, 1947), p. 140.

can do, the pictures that flash across his mind usually show ushers, Sunday-school teachers, deacons, janitors, superintendents, members of the board, and the committee in charge of the annual Christmas party. It is clearly an indictment of the Protestant churches of our time that one can be extremely "active" in a church by working on committees, preparing suppers, sorting rummage, or leading the youth group in recreation, and still have practically no understanding of the gospel or the mission of the Church universal.

Nearly every Protestant minister believes that laymen should be doing more than they are. Yet many ministers don't know how to get them activated, and many more don't know what to get them actively doing. This fact has always been a matter of deep concern for most Protestant bodies, but it is especially grave for any church that seeks to take its lay ministry seriously. The minister's problem is twofold: his job is to activate the membership but, equally important, he must get them busy doing Christian work and not busy-work.

Once again Elton Trueblood has given us the most wisdom about how to develop the lay ministry. He writes:

The universal ministry is a great idea, one of the major ideas of the New Testament, but the hard truth is that it does not come to flower except as it is nourished deliberately. Indeed the paradox is that the nourishment of the lay or universal ministry is the *chief reason* for the development of a special or partially separated and professionalized ministry. We cannot have an effective universal ministry of housewives and farmers and merchants simply by announcing it. It is necessary to *produce* it. The only way in which this can be done is by the education of a gifted few, whose chief vocation is the liberation of the ministerial and witnessing power of the many.[2]

[2] D. Elton Trueblood, *The Company of the Committed*, p. 63.

We have already said that the purpose of the pastor is to equip men for their own ministry. Here we must make clear that a *genuine lay ministry* is something more than church activity. Indeed, we already have too many ushers. John R. Mott, a pioneer in the ecumenical movement, once wrote: "A multitude of laymen are in serious danger. It is positively perilous for them to hear more sermons, attend more Bible classes and read more religious and ethical works, unless accompanying it all there be afforded day by day an adequate outlet for their new-found truth." [3] The minister as catalytic agent seeks to stir up a ministry of significance. One example of this has already been given in the preceding chapter, for to get people involved in the real redemptive work of a church is important work. However, much more than this alone is meant.

It may be that a radical and revolutionary rearrangement in traditional church organizations will be necessary before Christians can be stirred up. It may be that all of the standing committees which have been standing for so long will have to be junked and new groups formed solely on the basis of "concern" and a desire to act on the Christian impulses certain individuals have.

However, any pastor who is relatively bright and reasonably sober will realize that this will not happen very soon, if at all, in the established church. At any rate this radical rearrangement should not be necessary. It is the personnel and the attitude of a committee, not its structure, which ultimately determine whether it will perform a ministry of significance or not. For example, in one church in Indiana the decorations committee which under normal conditions existed simply to decorate the sanctuary on special occasions found itself composed of such capable persons who had such deep concern that it ended up

[3] Quoted in John von Rohr, "The Church: Minister or People?" *The Pulpit*, October, 1962, p. 15.

functioning as an evangelistic committee that brought many new persons into membership.

At any rate, within the traditional structure of the churches, the Christian pastor probably has at least one body through which he can work as a catalytic agent. This body goes under a variety of names, depending on the denomination: The Official Board, the Session, Vestry, Ministry and Counsel, or the Prudential Committee. The problem lies, however, in the psychological outlook of these groups. For the most part they are concerned with the church-institution and not its ministry. The idea that must be grasped is that the members of the key body of a church could comprise a ministering agent of exciting proportions. Already these people are responsible, interested people, or they would not be there. The minister's task is to get them interested in and responsible for the "right" concerns.

This is not easy, because too many of the groups are merely guardians of the "old ways," trapped by the habits of feeling concerned only about the physical upkeep of the building or the hiring of a new minister. These bodies are infrequently concerned about the mission of the church, but instead, see as their function the performance of certain traditional tasks. This is not as it should be. These church core groups should not reflect the "mean" or "average" attitude of a church. They should not be merely handlers of routine tasks, such as thinking up answers to this year's annual report. These ministering bodies should be far out in front of the rest of the congregation. Their job is not to reflect but to inspire. Every person who agrees to serve on this body should self-consciously regard himself as one appointed to be what is so scarce in Christendom today, namely, a *creative Christian.*

The minister, as catalytic agent, should work closely with such a group within the church. His relationship to that body is like that of a catfish to the cod, one who stirs up the others positively and actively to minister. This is the place to bring the concerns that he sees. This is the body which should react and respond to what the pastor has to suggest. He does not lay before them ideas and programs which they must accept-or-else (as if that would be possible with American Protestants!), but both he and the body should be psychologically ready to think, plan, propose, suggest, modify, change, improve, and reach out with a missionary-minded program.

One pastor, upon emerging from a boring and uninspiring session of his board, commented that if "our church is ever going to get anywhere, we should have at least one person on the board who is totally insane." We can see his point if we realize that radical Christianity in the local church is necessary, and the body which should produce it is that church's most responsible group. Hopefully, radical ideas will be wisely tempered, but our problem today is not that we have too much radical thinking. Our problem is that there is not enough.

A second way in which the Protestant pastor can stir up a ministry of his members is by functioning as a discoverer of talent. In nearly every Protestant church there are probably some who can preach. There are also many who cannot preach, and—fortunately—the idea of the universal ministry does not mean that every Christian should be able to do so. Still, there is no reason to think that preaching is the exclusive and special talent of the hireling minister. It is, instead, the responsibility of those who can do it reasonably well.

It is undoubtedly healthful for a church if a pastor does not do all of the preaching. Robert Raines tells of his experience in this regard when he writes the following:

When I am gone on a Sunday morning, the chances are good that one of our laymen will preach. In the last three years, twenty of our own laymen have preached on Sunday morning. During the

last calendar year, eight laymen preached. . . . Our laymen preach
the Sundays when I am on vacation in the summer. . . . [These
people] discover that they are meant to be ministers of Christ, like
the lay people described in the New Testament. When a layman
speaks of his own pilgrimage before the congregation, the people
listen and take heed as they seldom do when a professional clergyman says the same things.[4]

In the church which I presently serve, a similar experience has
been recorded. Over a period of months three different members prepared and delivered sermons. By and large these sermons were well received, although the congregation became no
more excited over them than over the regular pastor's sermons.
However, the fourth man delivered *an unusually helpful*
message. Upon his return, the pastor was greeted with the
joking (or so he assumed) remark that "we don't need you
anymore." This layman preached a sermon which aroused his
listeners. A talent had been discovered and several Christian
people had profited from one member's witness.

Another ministry, the talent for which is probably available
in nearly every Protestant congregation in America, is that of
selling and/or distributing Christian books. Sermons, speeches,
and talks communicate many Christian ideas better than those
in books, but there is one distinct advantage in getting someone
to buy a book; the buyer has invested something of value in
some ideas, whereas the message of a sermon is, in a sense,
"free." True, there is no guarantee that a person who buys a
book will read it, and we want to avoid the temptation to turn
the "temple" into a place where "money-changers" operate.
Nevertheless, a book table on which Christian books are at-
tractively displayed and which is provided and administered
by a qualified, concerned Christian can have a wide impact.

[4] *Op. cit.,* pp. 106, 108.

It might be astounding to some people if they realized how many people there are who are eager for help and who might buy a book on the subject but would not go to see a minister. Parents and young people who face the problem of interfaith marriage might well be exposed to James Pike's book, *If You Marry Outside Your Faith.* The little book by Leslie Weatherhead, *The Will of God,* has helped many already who ponder the meaning of life and death at the time of tragedy; someone who knows and loves books could make this slim volume available to many others whom a minister might never reach. Literally hundreds of other books could be distributed, also, and the pastoral ministry multiplied when a pastor discovers this talent among his members.

Another example is seen in what happened in a church located in a town with a serious slum problem. One of the problems which local social agencies in the community continually faced was the shocking lack of knowledge mothers had about the rudiments of child care, personal care, family relationships, and practical matters of sanitation and hygiene. Several Christian women—young married persons—in a church started a "mothers' club" out of which will come improvements in the standards of life for these people. This, of course, was not a case of discovering talent so much as it was a case of persons merely putting to use talents—in this case, talents in home economics —which they already had. The pastor in this instance merits no credit for the idea, but it serves as an illustration of some talents for which he could look and for which he might find some good use.

Sometimes an incidental comment will be a clue to a potential ministry which members of a church can have more fully if the implications of an opportunity are pointed out to them. In one small study group, for example, a woman commented that she and her husband were frequently being approached by young couples in their neighborhood who were having marital difficulties. They lived near some apartments which were usually occupied by young couples, and since they were better established residents, the younger people often came to them for advice. Already, it is clear, a ministry was being performed, but the potential for an even greater one was apparent. The couple possessed sensitivity, common sense, and a Christian concern. On one occasion they had served as a companion to a young person who needed professional help and thereby made it possible for that individual to have the courage to seek it. On other occasions they had called ministers and made arrangements for counseling interviews with troubled couples.

Here the pastor had an opportunity to establish a working, co-operative relationship. He could act as a catalytic agent to them by guiding them to one of the seminars that are available for laymen in fundamental counseling. He could even nurture their innate counseling abilities by helping them himself to learn some basic techniques. In these ways the pastor would be stirring up a ministry which would reach people whom the pastor-counselor himself might never reach. In his role as catalytic agent, the Protestant pastor will have to use his insight and creative abilities to discover opportunities for *practical witness* as well as using his sensitivity and perception to discover talents among the people he serves.

The job of the pastor is also to discover commitment. As we read the history of the church and the efforts of the founding fathers of most denominations, we sometimes feel that Christians "way back then" were united in their pioneering religious and humanitarian efforts. But this was seldom the case. More often than not one or two members of a church or even a denomination are out in front, setting an example or leading the way. Sometimes they are so far out in front of the rest of the church that they are mistaken as part of the enemy and consequently suffer alienation and rejection by the church itself. However, those few who have commitment and energy should be encouraged and guided by the pastor into significant action, even if the church at large rejects them. In every church there are probably a few who are or would be truly dedicated, committed Christians, if they were given impetus and guidance.

The pastor's responsibility is to search out such persons. His job is continually to throw out concrete challenges and opportunities to his congregation, and then nurture those who show real interest. Unless we have been deluding ourselves about the work of the Holy Spirit, there are those among us who would carry a cross or visit the prisons or counsel the lonely or do good to those who persecute them. The pastor's job is to find them, to give them an opportunity to express their commitment, and to the best of his ability equip them for their tasks. With them he must demonstrate that his is a kindred spirit, that he deeply understands and appreciates their desire to carry a cross even though he may not share the desire to carry their specific crosses.

A fourth area in which the pastor can serve as a catalytic agent is evangelism. A recent article by United Press International reporter Louis Cassels illustrates the dilemma regarding evangelism most Protestant bodies face.[5] He points out that it takes about sixty members with the help of ministers to add one new member to the church. This ratio is about the same in every major Protestant denomination. Cassels shows, too, that winning converts is not just a matter of proseletyzing people from one faith to another, in order to swell the membership statistics of a particular denomination. "There are more than 50 million people in America today who are not effectively related to any religious body. They constitute a vast mission field right under the noses of America's churches, and any

[5] Louis Cassels, "It Takes 60 or 279 to Win One," July 28, 1961.

Christian who takes his faith seriously must be concerned about proclaiming the Gospel to them."

The "hidden" fact about this statistic is not really very hidden at all. Sixty members are *not* now working to bring in one new member. More than likely, one member on the average is trying to bring in sixty. Yet, it is interesting to note that the solution suggested for this problem is "increased participation by laymen in the whole life of the church. . . . It [will be] characterized by a strong emphasis on the personal responsibility of every layman to serve as a bearer of the Christian message."

This conclusion is interesting, we say, because the early church was built on this premise, but we have either forgotten it or ignored it in recent years. The genius of any kind of evangelism is participation by the membership. One of the most serious signs of our present disease in the ministry is the psychological acceptance of the concept that it is the pastor's job to win new Christians. It is true that a poor preacher or a pastor with an offensive personality will undoubtedly add little to the ability of a church to gain members, but a good, concerned membership can transcend the liability of a poor pastor. If our earlier emphasis upon Christian community is sound, if this is the missing element from churches today, the reality of *koinonia* will be the major attraction to persons.

It is precisely for this reason that evangelism must be the primary responsibility of people-people, not pastor-people. The pastor's job of stirring up his membership to reach out is vital, because this is the only way a church can avoid the illusion that is so often given when evangelism is merely the pastor's job—namely, that the preacher is out drumming up an audience for his next public performance.

Whether pastors like it or not, the fact is that many—perhaps most—un-churched persons are conscious of a vested interest in the "professional" minister's approach to them. Again, this insight is not new, although it has never really been taken seriously by very many Christians or by very many pastors. Yet, person after person who has tried it has discovered that his call on a prospective member usually has more influence than the minister's. The chief reason for this is simply that the pastor is merely doing his routine work, whereas the laymen's interest in the person is assumed to be more sincere. The pastor is supposed to be *for* the church, much as the manager of the store is *for* the company, but the lay worker is credited with having more genuine conviction and friendship. Clearly, what we want to evangelize persons into is not an audience but a living fellowship. The attraction of this fellowship, this community, is not dependent upon professional smoothness or salesmanship. It depends instead on this very sincerity, genuine conviction, and personal interest of which we have spoken. It is not true, of course, that the layman *ipso facto* is a better evangelistic visitor than the minister. A great many willing laymen do their very best when on evangelistic missions to sound like preachers or at least like what they think preachers should sound. They often end up using even more pious and pharisaical language than the minister. Both the lay minister and the pastor must be clear in their own minds as to the reason and meaning of evangelism—that it is for the cause of Christ and not the cause of pastor X or layman Y or even the statistical success of the XY church. The pastor's job is to stir up and help interpret the meaning of the evangelistic enterprise among the members of his church.

An old idea, worth reviving, which the pastor could stimulate among his members is like that of the once popular program of "fireside evangelism." The kind of superficial "fellowship" of some social engagements is disheartening to many, yet the "right" people in the "right" circumstances can perform a ministry of hospitality which has important implications. One young couple has taken this idea very seriously and has made a matter of their personal stewardship to make their home available for meetings, contacts with new people, discussion of serious ideas, and a place where a visitor or even a stranger can find a welcome. The people involved enjoy this, and they do it well, yet it is a conscious effort on their part to perform an effort of Christian outreach. Most sophisticated Protestants would not be caught dead ringing doorbells for their church, but some undoubtedly would be congenial to a new idea. The key to its success is the spirit in which it is done, of course, and the effort will probably fail if it is carried on with a selfish motive, that of feeding friends in order to get them to join *our* church or go along with *our* ideas out of social obligation. Yet, this idea makes a ministry *of* the church *outside* the church possible.

Another way in which a pastor should act as a catalytic agent is in his administrative work with standing committees. Ask almost any honest pastor in almost any denomination and he will tell you that he works with the committees that have important work to be done. There is a lesson here that ministers must take seriously. If a pastor is very, very busy dashing to and from committee meetings, it is probably an indication not of personal dedication but of poor administration. He is an administrator in the worst sense. The minister who meets with key committees for important reasons is a far wiser man than the one who makes an appearance to "show his interest" although he has nothing tangible to contribute. Specifically, this means that he should not attend this meeting or that gathering simply because Mrs. Jones thinks it is "nice" for the pastor to be present. It should come to be understood that when the pastor appears, he comes bringing a suggestion for a new job that they should handle. Indeed, if this were the case, the invitations to the minister to "drop in" would rapidly decrease!

We have already talked about the importance of a responsible body doing creative work in a church. Another committee, often neglected, is the social order committee, although it, too, has a variety of names. In many congregations the idea of social action or mission work is limited to opposition to the opening of a new tavern or the sewing of loin cloths for natives in a foreign land. Yet, reaching out in service and witness is at the heart of the Christian witness. Unfortunately, many Christians are under the impression that to be for some kind of non-violent means of achieving peace or eliminating discrimination is vaguely disloyal. This means that many people do not take the functions of this committee seriously because of political reasons, not because of religious ones. Work in this area must take place in the context of *koinonia*, else the only thing the pastor will stir up is trouble.

The pastor must accept the humbling truth that there are a number of things that laymen can do better than he can, regardless of how much education and training to be a minister he may have had. For example, the responsibility in most cases for the physical plant should be dumped, lock-stock-and-barrel, into the laps of the congregation. If maintenance and expansion of the plant are not properly attended to, then let the bricks crumble and the termites gnaw away. There is a symbolic witness that needs to be made here, as the pastor demonstrates that his concern is not with the physical church building. Jesus may have been a carpenter, but his ministry was not preoccupied with carpentry.

Again, when a pastor finds a committee that is especially good and capable, he probably should let it alone. By and large if there is good rapport between a pastor and his people, they will seek out his help on the points where they need it. Otherwise the pastor will effectively be acting as a catalytic agent by staying out of the way. It is an unwritten law of religious work that the more responsibility a pastor assumes, the more a congregation will let him assume. It is probably wise that a minister never learn how to run a mimeograph machine or a movie projector, or at least he should not let people know that he can run them. This is not because he is too good or too far above such menial tasks; in fact, these instruments can be tools of a church's ministry. However, the point is that the minister has other functions to perform, and they require different tools and techniques.

Perhaps without knowing it always, some churches have been developing techniques and laboratories which the minister can use to stir up the ministry of his people. Some of these efforts for equipping the ministry are new; others have been in use several years.

For example, the "Indiana Plan" is a method of adult education to be used in the churches which has been developed by two Indiana University professors. The now famous Parish Life Conference of the Episcopal Church is designed to help persons think through the mission of the church in terms of the basic need of man. Church experiments like the Church of the Saviour in Washington, D. C., or the Peoples Church in Indianapolis, Indiana, or the East Harlem Protestant Parish in New York City offer the pastors models of churches which are people-centered rather than pastor-centered. The National Council of Churches sponsors a program in social action education in twenty-seven churches called "Operation Laity" in which pastors could be encouraging their people to participate. The Church of the Brethren, too, sponsors week long training in peace-making and a large number of conferences and seminars in social action are made available each year by the American Friends Service Committee. These are tools with which pastors can work as catalytic agents. One of the best ways of stirring up a ministry of significance is the development of Yokefellow Groups in the church. These groups explore and develop ways of promoting a ministry in depth in the local congregation.

Helps such as these are available to the pastor as he seeks to be a catalytic agent who stirs up a genuine ministry among congregations. When he can get his people involved in conferences and efforts such as these, when he is personally equipped to use the methods of this kind himself in the church, then he is about his proper business. The role of catalytic agent must come into proper perspective in the ministry. As Protestant pastors have sought guidance as to their particular responsibilities, they have adopted often not the role of catalytic agent but, instead, the role of a "busy-man-of-affairs." One of the minister's favorite recitals is to recount how many things he had to do in the course of any given day. They are all interpreted as professional activities, part of his job, things he must do. Yet, they are not catalytic activities; they are usually the activities of a "religious representative," who is attempting to demonstrate that religion is a full-time job.

How inaccurate this attitude is can be seen in a statement analyzing a report by the World Council of Churches which dealt with this very question. The analysis notes that in the deepest sense "the minister in clerical garb is not the best symbol of the church as a ministering community. Alongside this symbol," it says, "there is another figure":

This symbol is a layman, busy in the secular occupation by which he earns his livelihood. . . . He is in the world of daily work. . . . He wears the clothes that workers wear throughout the hours of the day and the days of the week—blue or white collars; overalls or business clothes; the special apparel of the operating room, of the conductor on the train, of the actor on the stage. . . . In him, the dedicated layman engaged in honest and useful employment, the Word is lived in concrete decisions and specific actions in the world.[6]

The pastor, as catalyst, can help provide concrete situations in which the layman will be able to minister.

The minister has certain advantages over the average member. He has the advantage of education (hopefully) and the advantage of time for continual study. However, the average member has certain advantages over the minister, too. He has the advantage of a less sheltered experience in many ways. Recently, *Time* magazine carried a story of a group of clergymen who visited an assembly line in a factory where they witnessed workingmen in action. They were amazed and disturbed by the boring, routine, and methodical work which these men were doing. The article concluded with some statements by the clergymen which said that they were going to have to re-think their theology in order to deal with the special problems of the industrial worker. The equipping minister, we like to think, would have a different response to such a "revelation." (We use the term "revelation" satirically because we cannot help but wonder where in the world these clergymen had been that this experience should be so new to them.) The Christian who works in a factory ought to have more knowledge about the relevance of faith to his job than the pastor has. The minister can share with the workingman a book on the subject, but he must also ask him the crucial question: "Does what this author has to say really speak to your condition?" Protestant ministers don't legislate morals and meaning *down* to people. It is far more important for the workingman to modify *his* theology to include his work than it is for the minister to modify his own thinking so as to make room for the workingman's

[6] Quoted by von Rohr, *op. cit.*, p. 15.

plight. More likely, people arrive at some part of the Truth by seeking together and sharing experiences. When the pastor can get members of his congregation to see this, he is fulfilling his role as a catalyst to their Christian experience.

As the Protestant pastor seeks to stir up a ministry among his people, his role is analogous to a man trying to direct and help others participate in a program of recreation. His job is not to put on an exhibition which people watch and possibly even cheer. Nor is it to get them out in the middle of the floor in order to feed him the ball while he scores. His job is to get them to play the game. When they throw the ball to him, he must fire it right back to them or to another teammate. He may score in some ways, but not always will he be the star. He may have to help some of the players learn how to play the game and develop their skills, but once they learn, he should let them alone to develop further on their own.

The Protestant pastor is not set free to be "busy" doing things as a representative of his congregation. He is set free to be busy getting other people to do things in the name of God. He is both leader and servant, part of the Body of Christ, yet not the entire body.

In short, the Protestant minister is not set free to be a busy-body. He is set free to get the Body busy.

chapter 5

The Pastor as Teacher

Although my mind is far from wise,
some of those who come to me make
astonishing progress. They discover
for themselves, not from me—and yet
I am an instrument in the hands of
God.

—SOCRATES

ONE OF THE CRUCIAL PROBLEMS OF OUR DAY FOR THE CONCERNED
Christian is illiteracy regarding the Judeo-Christian faith.
Knowledge of the Bible, for example, is pathetically small in
most Christian churches. Never before in our church history
have so many enrolled church members known so little about
the Bible. This problem of biblical illiteracy throughout Christendom is not due to a conscious rejection of Bible study. Most
Christians still cling to the idea that the Bible is a very good
thing to have around, and Americans are always a little proud
of the fact that the Bible is our number-one best seller each
year. Biblical illiteracy is the result of little serious study
of the Bible, and little serious study is given it because there

is an awareness of the difficulties involved in studying it, and there is the general impression that it and theology are simply not very interesting.

One Protestant minister, Thomas Roy Pendell, had been troubled for a long time by what he thought was biblical illiteracy among members of his church. Therefore, he decided to test his congregation one Sunday morning by giving them a simple quiz. "The results were staggering." He learned that

nearly one-fourth of the adult members of that Sunday's congregation could not identify Calvary as the place of Jesus' death. Over one-third did not know that Nazareth was the town where Jesus was brought up. "Gethsemane" rang no bell for 43 per cent, and "Pentecost" had no significance for 75 per cent. Only 58 per cent could identify the Gospels. . . . The median score of approximately 300 church attenders was still only 30 per cent. Twelve per cent could be said to have a good and five per cent an excellent knowledge of the Bible. But 83 per cent were essentially ignorant or at best are only sketchily acquainted with it.[1]

A Gallup poll revealed a similar degree of ignorance among the general public. It discovered that 51 per cent of the persons interviewed cannot name the first book of the Bible; 53 per cent cannot name even one of the four Gospels; 66 per cent do not know who spoke the Sermon on the Mount; and 79 per cent cannot name even one of the prophets of the Old Testament.

It should be clear that there is a great deal of learning that needs to be done by members of churches. We are not urging that people spend more time learning names, dates, and places of the Bible, but the nearly complete lack of knowledge of these things is probably an indication of a great lack of knowledge of

[1] Thomas Roy Pendell, "Biblical Literacy Test." Copyright 1959 Christian Century Foundation. Reprinted by permission from The Christian Century.

the main truths and ideas of the Bible as well. Furthermore, unless Mr. Pendell's church is by chance a Sodom in the midst of a land of righteousness—a highly improbable situation—the results in most churches on such a test would be very much like his. Indeed, one of the embarrassing reasons why the ecumenical movement is possible in our day is because most Christians in most denominations have at least one thing in common—mutual ignorance of basic Christianity.

It follows that if there is a need for learning, there is undoubtedly a need for teaching as well. The fact is, the simple gospel is often hard to understand. Harry Emerson Fosdick once said that the simple gospel is not nearly so simple as some simple people would like to believe. We live in an age in which skepticism about truth and authority is expressed with great abandon. In such an age an understanding of the history and meaning of the Bible is essential. Gone are the days when verses can be memorized and accepted—or rejected—on face value. Modern Christianity is composed of a hodge-podge of childhood memory verses, scientific method, positive thinking, the Declaration of Independence, and the underlying assumption that in this friendly freedom-loving land of ours religion belongs and we should somehow enjoy it.

Our faith is shallow when it needs to be deep. We live at a time when we cannot afford the luxury of wishy-washy Christianity and ignorance of the demands of the Living God upon us. Necessarily, then, the Protestant pastor must assume the role of teacher. It is no longer possible for preachers and speakers to water down the truth further than it has been diluted already. Before preaching will be either heard or taken seriously, there must be at least some common vocabulary and some common understanding of biblical and religious history.

Biblical illiteracy, as we have seen, cuts across denominational lines. Another area in which there is extensive ignorance among congregations is the knowledge of their own particular denominations. A common complaint in church after church is that people are essentially ignorant of the history and beliefs of their own Methodist, Presbyterian, Quaker, or other denomination. More than one person has come to a church and received the impression that you can be a member of that church and believe "any old thing," and it is common to hear a church member say that "it doesn't make any difference which church is yours because they're all trying to get to the same place." True, Protestants have much in common, yet the differences among them contribute to the richness and variety of witness which Protestantism has made over the years. However, it is easily possible to join a local church and become an active member in its many social activities without any understanding whatsoever of the history and beliefs of that church (or of Protestantism in general, for that matter).

This deficiency is not just in the area of *early* denominational history either. Not long ago, for example, one of the reading clerks in Indiana Yearly Meeting of the Society of Friends was heard over the public address system to ask: "What do the letters F-C-N-L stand for?" They happen to stand for the Friends Committee on National Legislation, one of the most significant denominational efforts Friends have! It is sad but true that in *most* churches there are probably not 10 per cent of the church population who could reasonably state why Jesus Christ is important to them. Before Christians can interpret and make their faith relevant to their daily lives, they will have to have some basic knowledge and understanding of what that faith is. The minister of the church should be the logical person to be their teacher.

This means that the Protestant pastor must plan to spend several hours of his time each week teaching and preparing to teach the members of his congregation basic Christianity. It

94

cannot be assumed that church members have absorbed this knowledge somewhere along the way in Sunday school or through a divine revelation on the way to worship. A far more accurate assumption is general lack of knowledge, or even worse, a distinct misunderstanding of Christian faith.

The role of the pastor as teacher is a sadly neglected one in Protestantism. In many churches the thought never enters the minds of their pastors that they should be teachers at all. That teaching is one of their prime functions is almost beyond their comprehension. The real sorrow of this situation is simply that the kind of training a minister has received is far more appropriate for teaching than it is for most of the functions he and his congregation usually expect him to perform. Most seminaries teach courses in Bible, theology, church history, ethics, sociology, and related subjects. However, in the local church the pastor frequently spends most of his time in business administration, mimeographing, fund-raising, and making public appearances. No wonder so many pastors feel their seminary education was irrelevant. No wonder so many theologians are asking themselves if seminary education really prepares their men for the local church. In actual fact, however, the teacher in seminary has usually instinctively known better what the local church needs than the so-called "experienced" pastor thinks he knows. The tragedy is that the pastor who does not teach spends most of his time doing things that he is absolutely not prepared to do, and wastes most of the knowledge which supposedly was gained in order to be an effective minister.

The pastor, in a very real sense, should be a teacher of teachers. With all its many faults, the Christian education program of the local church is the means through which will be communicated most of the religious knowledge that a young person receives in the church. No longer do perceptive Christians think that faith and commitment can simply be taught the way mathematics is taught and learned; but neither should the importance of the content and method of Christian education be discounted. Yet, for the most part, the Christian education of our children and our adults has been left in the hands of a few people, many of whom do not know what to teach or how to go about it.

Because of the general hodge-podge of ideas and information which is now being passed off as the content of the Christian faith, there should be a special responsibility for Christian education that is thought-provoking, stimulating, honest, and well-informed. Right now Christianity is often at the mercy of the personal prejudices and limitations of the teacher. It is not unusual to hear otherwise intelligent persons say that Christianity and Hinduism are about the same, except for the language differences. This shows an appalling ignorance of both Hinduism and Christianity. One teacher in a Methodist church used as his primary lesson material the abundant literature of the Masonic Lodge, of which he is an active and interested member. Too many teachers have failed to raise the "touchy" questions of religion—such as pacifism, the virgin birth, or specific forms of social action—simply because they personally have not faced these questions themselves. Yet if any real Christian witness can ever be the result of Christian teaching, the tough questions of ethics, faith, and theology will at least have to be raised. The pastor is the best person to raise them.

The knowledge of what faith is, of what the Bible is about, of what is not part of the Christian faith, and of what responsibilities for stimulating the consciences of their pupil teachers have—these matters should be directly communicated through courses taught by the minister. The assumption that a person will be a good teacher because he is willing, popular, and a good person is not valid. Christian education involves more than enthusiasm and good will. It involves knowledge, and a major part of the pastor's task is to help the willing teacher learn what and how to teach.

A second area in which the minister should function as a teacher is simply in the area of courses for the congregation in general. Whether or not those who attend these classes are going to be teachers, the effort to reduce the total amount of religious illiteracy among a congregation is an important one. A very practical but ambitious program which illustrates exactly the kind of teaching a pastor should attempt in the local church might include the following: (1) a course in the Old Testament; (2) a course in the Synoptic Gospels; (3) a study of certain books of the Bible in depth; (4) the "key" ideas of Christianity; and (5) the history of Christian thought.

In the teaching effort of the pastor, as he seeks to equip his people for their ministries, he can serve as a "counselor to counselors." Earlier we mentioned one example of how a pastor could help a couple to become marital counselors, but there are additional areas of "general counseling" which groups within the church can handle effectively—if they know how. Many competent pastors carry a heavy counseling load, and yet they often overlook the rich assistance which their congregations can offer.

Wayne Oates of Southern Baptist Theological Seminary has put strong emphasis on this point in his book on pastoral counseling:

Many of the people in a pastor's community are already depending upon each other for emotional aid and guidance. The pastor does not need to perceive himself as just a "counselor" to whom everyone must come. He cuts off the resources of the natural forces of helpfulness within a community itself should he insist on being *the* counselor. However, if he perceives himself as the pastoral guide of a purposeful fellowship of people who have a creative and redemptive intention toward each other, he can mobilize the resources of the whole community in both the prevention and the cure of some highly personal problems.[2]

There are many ways in which this idea can be implemented. One is for the pastor to hold informal get-togethers with parishioners who possess the necessary intelligence, sensitivity, and willingness to learn some techniques of counseling. Another is to use an already existing group, like a study group or even an adult Sunday-school class, which includes a number of individuals who have the proper qualifications. Still another way would be to encourage individuals to attend one of the lay centers of training wherein this kind of information and guidance is passed along, e.g., a Yokefellow Institute or a denominational school of the ministry for laymen.

The areas in which guidance could be given are not those that require specialized training. Indeed, the pastor would not, in most cases, be qualified to do this kind of teaching, and he should carefully avoid leaving the impression that either he or his people will be amateur psychiatrists once they have completed the course. There is, however, much that Christian people can do as counselors which will give content and direction to the redemptive concern of the local church.

One major area in which the pastor can work as a "counselor to counselors" is in dealing with the universal problem of grief. The church has long seen as its proper role that of being present and active at the time of death and crisis, but all who are familiar with the work of a local church can recall many occasions when a well-meaning parishioner has said or done things that hinder the readjustment of a grieving person more than they have helped. "It was the will of God," says a parish-

[2] From *Protestant Pastoral Counseling* by Wayne E. Oates. Copyright © 1962 by W. L. Jenkins. The Westminster Press. Used by permission.

ioner to a grieving mother who has lost her child; and if the mother believes this, it is obvious that the counseling task of the pastor is made greater, not less, because his parishioner gave misguided advice. If, however, a pastor can teach his parishioners the patterns and processes of the grief reaction, he will have given his church a big boost toward being truly a fellowship of the concerned.

An excellent aid in this effort is Granger Westberg's little book, *Good Grief,* which is inexpensive and easily understood, two characteristics that make it an ideal tool for teaching lay Christians. Many Christian people are eager for such knowledge because they have frequently been placed in situations in which they wanted to show comfort and concern to a grieving person but just didn't know how to go about it, especially when faced with the hard question, "Why did this happen to me?" The pastor who helps prepare his people for their counseling roles helps himself, his church, and surely those who seek comfort and help at the time of loss.

Another aspect of counseling which can be taught or caught is the basic stance of listening. We live in a world in which people talk a lot but do not listen carefully to what another person is saying. A few pastors have held what they have called "self-understanding" groups in their churches, and these have been quite helpful in teaching people to hear what another human being is saying and, possibly, sense the feelings that go with his words. Essentially this is the context of counseling, and it is a basic attitude which lay Christians can provide as adequately as a pastor. It is an attitude of listening, in other words, which can be developed and nurtured—if a pastor will include such groups in his educational program.

It would probably be helpful, too, if a minister from time to time would confront his people with some of the signs of mental illness which they would be in a position to observe.

Sunday-school teachers, for example, are often in a better position to observe these signs than the pastor—if they have eyes with which to see them. A physician in an Indiana mental hospital attributes his cure and subsequent release to the loving concern of local Christian men who established a pattern of visiting in the mental hospital. These men did not try to be amateur psychiatrists, but they proved the redemptive power of genuine personal concern. So many times, furthermore, a pastor feels that he, alone, understands and is sensitive to the psychological needs of individuals and families. He lacks confidence in the layman's ability to handle such people and problems, and often there is good reason for his lack of it. However, our day is one in which counseling is an important form of ministry, and the burden of its responsibility is too great to bear alone. For the sake of his church and his own mental health, the pastor must become a counselor of counselors.

So important is this kind of intensive Christian education that it is not surprising to learn that it lies at the center of the program of some of our most exemplary churches. One of the few truly encouraging Christian churches in our time in terms of commitment and depth of witness is the Church of the Saviour in Washington, D.C. It is important to see that its program of Christian education is a continuing one, carried on weekdays and week-nights, and—especially relevant for our consideration—the main teacher of these courses is Gordon Cosby, the pastor of the church. He has help, to be sure, but most of his help comes from people he has trained.

One of the major aspects of study with which the pastor should confront his people in the educational program of his church is that of the nature of the church and its ministry. Indeed if more Christians were aware of the mission of the church, there would be less misunderstanding of what the church ought to be doing today. A class about the ministry, too, would be in order, as more layman might become aware of what the pastor's real task is—namely, equipping them for ministry.

One Episcopal rector travels throughout the diocese to which he belongs concentrating primarily on this one fundamental question: What is the church? Such concentration is necessary because most church members in most denominations do not know, or at least they have a misguided understanding of what it is. It may well be a "treasure in an earthen vessel," but most congregations are preoccupied with the vessel rather than the treasure. Extensive teaching about the doctrine of the church must be high on the pastor's list of priorities. Perhaps if ministers and laymen can learn what their mission is, they will be able to carry it out.

A third area in which the minister should function as a teacher is in the Sunday-school itself. Ideally, the group with which he deals would be the class which is most clearly the "growing edge" of the church. If it is a class of young married people which seems to have the best chance for potential religious growth, one of the major responsibilities of the pastor would be to make this class as attractive, stimulating, and challenging as he can. Once again we have the problem of too many pastors who give the impression that they are too "busy" to teach a class. Such pastors, to put it briefly, are wrong. Other ministers say, too, that they cannot properly put themselves into the appropriate mood for their preaching if they must also teach a class on Sunday morning. These men are probably making two mistakes at the same time. They are underestimating the importance of this teaching opportunity, and they are probably overestimating the results which come from their preaching. Under normal conditions, more Christian growth probably results from a live discussion of Truth than from an oration about Truth.

Harold F. Carr has given us a good insight into how the

101

teaching atmosphere lends itself to appropriate Christian instruction:

> The minister kindles through friendship, testimony, and teaching an alertness and eagerness for the truth. He does more than instruct, inform, and pronounce the teaching of the Bible and the Church. He does not give the impression that his words must be accepted as final and complete.
>
> This Christian approach as adopted by the Protestants is admittedly more difficult. The educator stays in the class. He sits at the table, not on a raised platform. He is not, as someone said, "eight feet above contradiction," as when in the pulpit. He may be more advanced in knowledge and experience and thus able to guide the search. He is still the comrade in looking for the better way to live.[3]

Mutual study and class discussion allows for involvement to a far greater degree than the spectator sport of sermon-listening.

Another teaching function often overlooked by ministers is the opportunity to use effectively the program period at the many clubs, banquets, and gatherings at which he is invited to speak. How wearily the club president must introduce Pastor Jones of First Church who is speaker for the day. Club members are weary of the Pastor Joneses of whatever denomination because they know within themselves that the good pastor is either going to give a sermonette on what a real he-man Jesus was or show his slides of the Holy Land. On his part Pastor Jones is a little weary, too, because he knows that his well-fed audience is expecting to be bored. So, resignedly, he quickly throws together a couple of illustrations from the 1962 edition of *Sermon Stories with a Point,* adds a joke or two, and a concluding poem, and then hurries home to get next Sunday's bulletin run off.

[3] Harold F. Carr, "The Minister's Work as Religious Educator," *The Ministry,* ed. J. Richard Spann (Nashville: Abingdon Press, 1949), p. 110.

Why must this be? Here is a remarkable opportunity to teach. The Rotarians or the Ladies' Guild have their defenses up and are well prepared to resist preaching, however good it may be. They will be glad to hear the good minister tell some funny stories, with or without points, but this really accomplishes nothing. How much better it would be to lead a discussion on race relations, or give a talk on capital punishment, or sponsor a panel of club members on the "Moral Problem of the Movies." One of the best programs I ever sat in on was in a Rotary Club which discussed the reasons for its own existence. There are so many ideas for teaching subjects for groups like these that it is a wonder why they have been overlooked. The minister should leap on these opportunities every time one appears.

The minister can teach, too, outside the church through interdenominational efforts. In communities of many sizes there is usually the opportunity for co-operative classes for laymen. The pastor's job is to encourage them to be started and, if possible, to teach them. Most churches on their own do not have enough young people getting married each year to sponsor classes in preparation for marriage. Together, however, several churches could co-operate in this effort, and certainly it is desperately needed. The pastor who realizes the value of Christian teaching will not only take advantage of teaching opportunities, he will also help to create them.

Finally, there is another area in which Protestant pastors will someday have to be busy teaching. Surely many Christians are disturbed by the fact that religious education in the high-school years does not get the same serious attention as the regular academic subjects of the school system. This is unavoidable, of course, because of the separation of church and state. Equally disturbing, however, are the standards and values which are apparent in many public (and private) schools and which are essentially pagan. The tremendous emphasis on athletics at the expense of scholarship, the casual acceptance of extravagant expenditures for social events, and the high-pressure involvement of students in busywork are some of the matters which make some Christians wish that their children were able to get something better.

Church-related preparatory schools are available, of course, but they are expensive and many parents hesitate to send their teen-age sons and daughters off to a school hundreds of miles away. A parochial system, such as that of the Missouri Synod Lutherans, is effective, but such a system will not soon be established by most denominations. Still, something must be done. Someday the Protestant minister will have to function as the teacher of an after-school class which will be treated with respect equal, at least, to that afforded by students in their high-school courses. Perhaps the Protestant minister could be the key figure in the restoration of the serious study of Christian faith and practice. Certainly, if the ability to teach such courses were one of the criteria by which a pastor were hired and his work evaluated, this would put the responsibility for teaching in proper perspective in the work of the Protestant minister.

At the moment, however, before the role of teaching can be restored to its rightful place in the church, there are some prerequisites which must be met. There is, in the first place, a very clear implication which must be taken seriously. To be a teacher one must have a better-than-average grasp of religious truth and insight. In short, he must have as much education as he can get. Education in and of itself does not prepare men for the equipping ministry. Going to college and then to seminary certainly does not guarantee the eventual product of a good pastor. However, a contrasting conclusion that far too many Christians have drawn is even less true. Some Christians espouse the weird idea that not getting a theological education somehow does ready one for the pastorate.

The brutal fact is, unfortunately, that one of the reasons why Protestant pastors have not accomplished a great deal is simply a lack of preparation. The kind of intellectual discipline expected of men entering the ministry usually does not compare to that expected of men entering a field such as law or medicine. Yet should Protestant pastors return to the task of teaching truth instead of vaguely representing it, their intellectual grasp of Christian faith and practice will have to be greater than ever before. In Protestantism, wherein a pastor has no "built-in" priestly prestige or status, the gospel has to stand on its own feet *and the actual interpretation the minister brings to it.* What the minister teaches will not be accepted or taken seriously simply because *he,* even though an ordained minister, says so. The gospel he interprets will have to be presented forcibly and dramatically because those to whom he presents it will not accept it just because he vouches for its importance. The Pope may speak *ex cathedra;* the Protestant minister must appeal to reason, to the Scriptures, to the light within, to tradition, to knowledge, to truth as he understands it. His chance of being an effective Christian teacher will be far better if his understanding is great.

A first-rate religious education is necessary for the minister, too, simply because the people with whom he deals are better educated themselves now than ever before. The day is gone when the village preacher was probably the best educated man in town. Nearly all Christian ministers are familiar with the intellectual—pseudo or real—who looks down his nose at the "sentimentality and lack of depth" of the Church. More serious than this man, however, is the problem of the searching young man or woman who may be for the first time asking serious religious questions.

Warren Ashby in the *Christian Century* makes an important statement concerning this very problem:

Is the Protestant church dealing adequately with the religious situation of the college student of today? This vexing question occurs again and again to anyone seriously concerned for both university and church, since the future of both institutions and of many students will be shaped in part by the answer. The answer is being written right now in the experience of many individuals, but no one yet knows with certainty what it will be. There is, however, much evidence that the Protestant church is failing college students at a time of unique transformation in their lives.[4]

If this man's judgment is accurate, and it probably is, one of the reasons why the failure is taking place is that the local church and the local minister are not able to meet the intellectual doubts of the student. Because the agnostic professor of psychology or biology is smarter and better educated than the pastor (who has had two years of college and an extension course in the Letters of Paul) , the case for the Christian gospel is not given equal time by the student.

The Christian pastor needs an education, then, the best education he can get. Certainly if he plans to teach, he must be prepared to do so. His education will not in itself make him an effective minister, but his lack of it may very well keep him from being one. If he is not prepared intellectually for his task, he will be unable to guide persons whose intellectual difficulties stand between them and spiritual growth.

A second implication of this emphasis on teaching by the minister is that the pastor must discipline himself by continual study and reading. The educated man, and certainly the educated pastor, is not done when his beloved *alma mater* hands

[4] Warren Ashby, "Protestant Church and College Students." Copyright 1960 Christian Century Foundation. Reprinted by permission from *The Christian Century*.

him his diploma. On the contrary, the A.B. or Ph.D. degree he receives should really mark the beginning of his education. If he is fortunate, college and seminary will give the pastor an incentive and the tools with which to improve himself.

It would undoubtedly be embarrassing to discover how many ministers in every denomination are preaching sermons from canned outlines, boring their listeners with old clichés about Christianity which no longer have any real meaning, and decorating their walls with books which serve more nearly the function of wall paper than resource material. To a certain extent many ministers feel almost guilty about spending their "working time" reading and studying because they think their congregation expects them to be "doing something" for the church of their choice. This, however, is just another reason why teaching must become an explicit role of the Protestant pastor, so that *preparation for* teaching will be regarded as acceptable and necessary to his role.

A final prerequisite which must be fulfilled if the minister is to be a teacher of Christian truth concerns the program which he promotes. There is only so much time in the day, and in the mind of most church members there are just so many hours that will be devoted to formal church work. Thus, if the minister is to function as a teacher, he will probably have to make very clear that this effort has a high priority in the total church program. It will have to be made clear that the minister regards Christian education as more important than some of the rummage sales, teas, circle meetings, and gossip gatherings that have nothing to do with Christian education.

Setting up a nicely organized program of Christian education to be led by the minister will not automatically mean that church time will be properly used. Nevertheless, if young men and women who want to do significant Christian work can see and understand that teaching persons is part of their task, that task becomes sharper, clearer, and more important. If Christianity is to escape the burden of its generalized and shallow condition, serious teaching and serious learning by Christians who are serious about their faith will have to occur. If ministers are to help persons become disciples, they will have to first become teachers themselves.

chapter 6

The Man of Truth

*He who begins by loving Christianity bet-
ter than Truth will proceed by loving his
own sect or church better than Christianity, and end in loving himself better than
all.*
—SAMUEL TAYLOR COLERIDGE

ANY PERSON IN PUBLIC LIFE HAS DIFFICULTY IN SEEING HIMSELF
as others see him. Ministers are no exception, and it may
even be that they have greater difficulty in being objective
about the actual image they present to others because they
usually receive much more direct praise from their congregations than they do direct criticism. Yet, there is reason to believe that ministers are not always as loved or lovable as they
think. In a letter to the columnist Ann Landers, one disgruntled
ex-churchgoer writes:

Dear Ann Landers:
Whenever you get a problem too tough to handle you say "See
your clergyman." I quit going to church eight years ago and I don't
know any clergymen because I don't travel in the right circles. The
clergymen in this town are too busy getting their pictures in the

paper to bother about helping people. Why should they visit the sick or listen to people's troubles when they can collect a fat fee for making a speech to a woman's club or burying somebody rich? The dedicated servant of God is a thing of the past, Ann, so stop telling people to see their clergyman. Clergymen don't want to be bothered. (signed) Wised Up.[1]

There is the temptation simply to regard such feelings as these as so many sour grapes. Certainly we would not regard this man's attitude toward ministers as typical.

Nevertheless, one of the hard facts which ministers in every denomination must face is that today a large number of people are suspicious of the preacher's motives. There is a growing attitude of anti-clericalism in America today, and not all those who share it are angry young (or old) men like the example cited above. There may have been a time when the typical pastor was a symbol of deep dedication, self-sacrifice, and hard-working humility. However, that image is held by fewer people today than in the past. Should ministers sit anonymously in barber shops, locker rooms, hospital waiting rooms, and many other places where the subject of ministers and the ministry incidentally comes up, they might be astounded. Today many pastors are assumed to have ulterior motives for the work they do in the name of their churches. Many assume that ministers are persons who feel the world owes them a living. Partly because of the scientific-minded age in which we live, hucksters of religion don't seem to be performing any necessary services. They are sometimes even regarded as "free-loaders" who don't have to "work" for a living.

We cannot overemphasize that this attitude is largely the result of the time in which we live. We are passing through a period in which faith is a very good thing to be on record

[1] Courtesy Ann Landers, and Publishers Newspaper Syndicate.

110

as having, although not very important. We are now entering a new period, say many sociologists of religion, in which easy acceptance of religion is being transformed into actual antagonism toward religion. We are entering the post-Christian era. No doubt this changing attitude is one of the reasons why fewer men than before are entering the pastoral ministry.

However, in embarrassed honesty we must face another fact: There is reason to be suspicious of motives and actions of the professional clergy, regardless of denomination. As those who are skeptical and even not-so-skeptical look at pastors, preachers, and priests, some of the practices and attitudes they see give weight to this judgment.

One thing they see over and over again is a group of persons who seem to expect special privileges. The traveler hears the clergyman asking for "clergy rates" on trains and now on planes. The businessman sees him buying his clothes at a special discount "for wearers of the cloth." In some places he is given, and comes to expect, free membership in the country club, or a service club, or the Y.M.C.A.

It is not hard to find, either, a spirit of jealousy and competition with other ministers and other churches. The minister in many cases is regarded as a "denominational pusher," a man who is not nearly so interested in increasing the followers of Christ as he is in increasing the followers of himself.

Most people have come to assume that the pastor should be paid for special services. It is not uncommon to hear a clergyman make the ghoulish complaint that he got "only five dollars for the last funeral." The figure of "marryin' Sam," too, is a figure which flashes through the minds of many when weddings take place. Some ministers eagerly anticipate being located in a community near a state line in order to get more weddings of transients and elopers. No wonder one of the holiest of occasions is becoming lost in commercialism.

It is easy to find, also, many ministers who are quite jealous of their titles and hypersensitive to the signs of status which they are sure they deserve. The title "reverend" and how it should properly be used has been the subject of more than one article in ministers' magazines. May the saints preserve the poor sinner who makes up a church bulletin which lists the guest speaker for the day as merely "reverend" when he should have been called "the reverend doctor!"

Apparent on many occasions, furthermore, is a "professional" attitude toward the church ministers serve. Just as organization men think of one job as a stepping-stone to another, better job, so congregations are beginning to wonder why the mysterious "call" to service in another church invariably seems to send their pastor to a bigger church and a better salary. The man who goes to a small church frequently regards his service there as a kind of internship before he moves on to a better-paying position.

Undoubtedly, the average wage for ministers in most denominations would still be miserably low if pastors themselves had not complained about it. Certainly in some denominations there is still some complaining to be done. Yet, those looking on do not have to search far in order to find pastors who are preoccupied with getting what's coming to them. The minister often seems to be preoccupied, in other words, not with preaching the gospel at any cost but with the wages for preaching against sin.

It is sad but true that if we wanted to describe a clergyman and emphasize the corruptions of his role, a number of real-life examples come to mind. This is not to say, of course, that taking a fee for a funeral service automatically denies the sincerity and sympathy of the officiating pastor. The point simply is that when *all* the overtures and hints of insincerity, ulterior motives, special privileges, and private ambitions are put together, it is not difficult to see why many suspect the dedication and devotion of pastors as a group.

There is a growing feeling of resentment in the minds of many as they observe the pastoral ministry, furthermore, simply because the life of the pastor seems "soft" and easy. There is no time clock to punch, and no boss to whom he must report daily. If a man is intellectually inclined, the ministry offers opportunities for study and reading that other men, similarly inclined may not be able to enjoy. It is common for ministers to take lengthy trips to see the world, and what community does not have at least one minister who has visited the Holy Land. The minister may enjoy the isolation from the competitive struggles of society that others cannot have. It is not difficult, in fact, to see why many could come to resent ministers as a group.

Every serious Christian, and especially the minister, is open to judgment on this score, whether he merits criticism or not. He is open to it because of the nature of the gospel he proclaims. Sacrifice, commitment, discipleship, love—these are fundamental to his faith, and the moment a man's practice deviates from a reasonable adherence to them, in that moment his motives become suspect.

The question we must face, however, goes below the surface of the ministerial image. We must not confuse the smoke with the fire. Is the problem of the ministry today merely one of ignorance by the local pastor as to what his role is or ought to be, or is it also a question of a distortion by the minister of his own self-image? If the problem is just a superficial one, then we pastors can simply refuse to accept a few honoraria and turn down a clerical discount or two and perhaps the disgruntled will one day think better of us.

Yet this brings us to our central concern. The minister's task is not just to give a better impression. He must *be* a man of truth, and then let a better impression flow from that different being. Even if a pastor *understands* that his primary role is to be that of equipping others for their ministry, he must then confront himself with the hard question: is this who I *want* to be? To be a "builder of community," a "catalytic agent," and a "teacher" is to be in specific ways a servant, and to be a servant will require real self-understanding by the pastor.

There is, for example, an aura of mystery that surrounds the work of the minister in his role as counselor. There is a certain exclusiveness, a certain occult power, accorded the pastor as he functions as a personal counselor. It is much like the awe which the layman holds for the psychiatrist, as he regards him as one holding priestly powers and possessing highly technical skills. Will the pastor be willing to sacrifice some of this special status by sharing the "mysteries" of counseling as he teaches others to become counselors to some degree in their own right? Doubtless, some pastors are offended by the idea that, say, a barber could do as effective job of counseling in some circumstances as they could.

If a pastor takes seriously his task as a discoverer of talent, how jealous can he be of his preaching ability? There is a terrific temptation for ministers to regard the pulpits of *their* churches as *their* pulpits. True, on Layman's Sunday it is easy to stand back graciously and let John Smith, the local butcher, take over. On a more frequent basis, however . . . ah, that is the question! In fact, the pastor even has to face the fact that some of his members will probably think he is lazy in seeking to nurture the speaking skills of some of his members. Will he be willing to risk this?

Another special temptation of the minister is to enjoy the image of one's self as an administrator. The intensity of the temptation can be seen by noting the results of a recent survey. In drawing up a psychological task for seminaries for the Rockefeller Foundation program, the Educational Testing Service sent a questionnaire to one thousand lay leaders in various denominations, asking them to mention adjectives and to give profiles that represented their own concept of "an outstanding minister." This data was then turned over to another group of psychological testers. These testers were asked, "Who do you think is being described?" Their answer: "A junior vice-president of Sears-Roebuck." [2] It is currently in vogue to criticise the busyness and the overorganization of the churches and the time-consuming administrative work of the minister, but there is the real possibility that many pastors very much like things the way they are. Subconsciously they may like being regarded as a junior vice-president of a corporation. Many ministers, especially the most "successful" ones, may delight in the self-image of themselves as men behind a desk, dictating letters to a furiously writing secretary, greeting the people who (he may insist) *come to him,* and spending hours tied up with "important" phone calls. In words, there is real opportunity for the contemporary pastor to be a manipulator of persons, and manipulation implies having a personal power *over* people that ultimately causes them to be dependent upon him.

The minister runs another risk too. Many men who enter the ministry make great initial financial sacrifices in terms of serving tiny churches and paying for their seminary education. Later the idea of "moving up" to a more affluent life is regarded as both natural and deserved, as a kind of reward for earlier sacrifices. Yet this attitude lays a minister wide open to the temptation of using the ministry for personal achievement. Paradoxically, the ministry never gets poorer than when it grows rich.

An illustration of this fact can be seen in a recent article in

[2] Zimmermann, *op. cit.,* p. 117.

Time magazine in which the subject of "Pastoral Pay" is discussed.[3] The article points out that ministers generally are beginning, at least, to share with their congregations in the national affluence. The average minimum pay for priests in eighty-five parishes in an Episcopal diocese in Ohio is now $8,000.

In the American Baptist Convention, the average ministerial salary (including housing allowance) has risen from $3,903 to $5,795 during the past decade; since 1956 the number of pastors earning $10,000 or more has tripled. Last April the United Lutheran Church in America announced that since 1955 the number of its clergymen earning less than $3,000 had dropped from 182 to 20; the number earning $10,000 or more rose from eleven to 85.

When fringe benefits are added to base salary, too, it is obvious that there is abundant opportunity to do well by doing good.

What makes the above statistics significant, however, is the revealing attitude which accompanied them. One Presbyterian minister in Detroit, the article pointed out, refused to accept a new call until the church agreed to "cough up an extra $4,000." The president of the Church Federation of Los Angeles is quoted as saying that "most of the fellows I know who are underpaid are incompetent. They couldn't make it better anywhere else." The *Time* article concluded with this especially revealing comment:

Churchmen in mainstream Protestant denominations agree that capable young pastors can indeed work their way up without much difficulty. "The church is like any other profession," says the Rev. Magee Wilkes, 44, a vice president of the Southern California School of Theology. "The best men make the most money. Churches are willing to pay for leadership." [4]

[3] September 14, 1962, p. 80. Courtesy *Time;* Copyright Time Inc., 1962.
[4] *Ibid.*

The minister who regards the ministry "like any other profession" is leaving himself wide open for a distortion of his proper role. He finds himself faced with the subtle but real temptation to "work his way up" when he should, instead, be asking himself how he can serve God and man best *in the community where he is at that moment.* The call to service in another field is not the same as a call to a better deal.

As the pastor considers his self-image, he must even confront himself with his own basic personality, with his motivations and emotional attitudes. What does he really think of people? Why, after all, did he choose to go into the ministry? Superficiality in personal relationships possibly could be the result of a too-long working day, or it could be that a pastor thinks his real personality and his pastoral personality are somehow separate. Nolan B. Harmon has commented on this kind of ministerial schizophrenia in these words:

> We have known men of the ministry who had been so schooled and trained to act as they had seen older ministers act for so many years, that they seemed artificial, stiff, and stilted in everything they did. They walk into a restaurant as though they are mrching into the Sunday morning pulpit, and greet their friends as though they are glad-handing all comers at the door of the church.[5]

The "real man" must be the one who goes into the ministry, not the "other" self who is a facade of Sunday-school manners and professional mannerisms that he thinks are appropriately ministerial. There are probably many in the ministry today who are trying to hide behind time-honored phrases, ecclesiastical vestments, and pulpit protection. Yet the inadequacy of their own self-image of the ministry has been a contributing factor to the distortion of society's image of it. Every man or

---

[5] Nolan B. Harmon, "His Ethics," *The Ministry, op. cit.,* p. 148.

woman who enters the ministry must know who he is, what his motivations are, what he actually thinks of his fellowman, and what his special temptations are.

Thus, because of the conditions of our century and because of the witness which Christians need to make, the Protestant pastor will have to demonstrate that he *is* a "man of truth." There are many things which we have said a minister must do; here we are concerned with what he must *be*. He must be something different not because he is special, but because his temptations are special. To be a minister carries with it responsibilities which affect who a man is.

If a minister is going to be a "man of truth" in our day, his motives will be beyond suspicion by any reasonable man. It also means that the unfortunate image which we have described, the sad composite of doubtful acts and attitudes, will be challenged and confronted again and again. A minister who is a "man of truth" will be an "image-buster." Therefore the Protestant minister will necessarily stop being the local "prayer boy" at public functions. When asked to bless the food (and thereby get a free meal), he can gently refuse with the suggestion that the blessing would mean much more if one of the "non-professionals" did the praying. When the undertaker slyly edges up to the minister before or after the funeral with a ten-dollar bill concealed in his palm, the pastor can either refuse or turn the money over to the church to buy a suitable memorial for the deceased.

When it comes to buying things, ministers will have to do as many other Americans have to do, namely, wait for sales and bargains. They should never accept clerical discounts by virtue of their status. Things are so bad on this score, in fact, that they should probably make purchases elsewhere if discounts to ministers are store policy. Surely, too, it is time we ministers make some quiet protests to those many fine citizens who insist that they call us "reverend." It is true that if every minister took to task every person and agency which referred to him in this way, he would get nothing else done. Who knows? If the use of "reverend" went out of style, those who cut our hair and sell us groceries and service our car would have to remember our names just as they have to do for "real folks"! Theological differences will cause the use of "reverend" to vary, but the minister himself should never place great emphasis upon its use.

When the nearly inevitable invitation comes for him to join a service club as chaplain, the minister's conscience should be his guide. Always the expectations of the job must be considered. If to be chaplain means to be the club "holy man," the giver of the blessing, the symbol of religion, then he should refuse. Certainly he should pay his way whatever the conditions; the chaplaincy does not entitle him to free meals. The main justification for even taking the job would be to use the position as a means of getting some significant programs onto the agenda.

It goes without saying, of course, that these protests be made with as little self-righteousness and as tender a spirit as the minister can muster. Always there is the temptation to be legalistic about such things by setting up inflexible rules that, as a cure, may be worse than the sickness. There are some persons who give gifts to a minister, not because his status as a minister "demands" such gifts, but because they are kind and generous people who give gifts to ministers, doctors, paper boys, and many other persons. Many persons give gifts to doctors, not because of their status, but out of gratitude for the *persons* they are. To reject gifts of this kind would be to let the letter rule the spirit of the law.

Protestant pastors will have to use their heads and their hearts in their efforts to demonstrate the truth. Nevertheless, it must be done. These gentle protests are nearly unavoidable because

119

individual ministers will be confronted by numerous opportunities to conform to the stereotype we have deplored. It is the minister's responsibility to make this protest because he is the most logical person to demonstrate that a clergyman has no special access to God. He, of all people, should not recognize artificial distinctions among men. If enough ministers truly are and behave as "men of truth," a new and better stereotype of the pastor will be shaped of which we can be proud. If the concept of the priesthood of all believers is a true concept, then we must reject the perversions of this idea that have become apparent in the image of a clergyman.

Another way in which a Protestant minister can demonstrate that he is a man of truth has to do with what he says and how he says it. We must recognize again that this concern cuts across denominational lines. The fact is that there are a number of ministers who do not wear clerical garb, who may protest clerical abuses, but still set themselves apart from—and by implication—above other Christians. They employ "holy language" in sermons, in conversations, in teaching, and in many other places which is more of a hindrance to communication than a help.

The testimony of simplicity needs to apply to what we say as well as to how we live. One of the tragic facts is that with the great abundance of sermons, talks, and lessons that are given in churches, only a small part of their content is being listened to and understood. Much of the blame for this rests on the shoulders of the one who is doing the talking—our friend the minister. A pastor is not really speaking the truth unless he is willing to be understood, willing to work at real communication. A recent newspaper article speaks our mind in this regard:

There are millions of people in America today who have had the Christian gospel preached at them—but not to them. . . . They are

victims of a break down in communication between the church
and the modern world. . . . One big reason why the church is not
getting its message across is that it speaks too often in jargon. Web-
ster defines jargon as "technical, esoteric or secret vocabulary of a
special group." That's a fair description of the language—compounded of venerable theological terms and biblical phrases—
which the church is likely to use when it tries to explain to modern
man why Jesus of Nazareth is the most important thing that ever
happened to the human race.[6]

This, obviously, is another indication why the Protestant pastor
should be a carefully educated person. His education ought
to point out to him that preaching and talking about the gospel
is an extremely difficult task. Unfortunately, too many pastors
feel that the acquisition and use of certain well-worn clichés
and pet "holy phrases" is preaching. They fail to recognize
that unless the gospel is actually communicated, it will be
totally ineffective as "good news."

This problem of saying what we mean is a problem for ministers in all denominations. There is no reason to believe that
simple, direct, clear, and straightforward communication is
more characteristic of ministers in one denomination than in
another. Nevertheless, as men who go on record as full-time
ministers, clergymen must find and use words and metaphors
which expose the gospel, not disguise it.

While we have suggested that education is a means of helping
ministers communicate, this is certainly no guarantee that plain-
ness of speech will be the result. In fact, as every professor of
homiletics knows, education can confuse and lend itself to a
real lack of communication. Perhaps there is no better illustration of the error which the Protestant minister ought to seek
continually to avoid than what the late Halford Luccock de-

[6] Louis Cassels, "Book Bypasses Churchly Jargon," *Indianapolis News*, Friday,
March 24, 1961.

scribed in one of his best-known columns, entitled, "If I Were Satan." In this article Dr. Luccock says that if he were Satan and wanted to defeat the power of the gospel:

> I would give most of my attention to getting a job as a professor in a theological seminary, possibly a professor of Unsystematic Theology, and teach the boys a whole dictionaryful of long dense words that nobody could understand. I can't think of any better way of making void the word of God, and I'll bet Satan can't think of any either.
>
> I thought of that idea the other Sunday when we had a fine young minister preach at St. John's. He will be a good man when he gets over this obsession with foreign jargon. It's like getting over measles or whooping cough. I can't tell you about the high spots of the sermon. Even the low spots were out of my reach. It was something about the correlation of the kerygma and epistemology —that is, presupposing the universality of the logos. But there seemed, he said, to be an imbalance of subjective and objective data which prevents methodological research. There was also something to do with the existential involvement which had a bad effect on eschatology.[7]

Surely this is ample illustration of what the user of words must avoid! The purpose of this book is not to give instruction in preaching; this in itself is a large matter to consider. However, it is important to emphasize the built-in obligation which a Protestant minister should accept, namely, to speak the truth in a way that can be understood. The minister will have to ask himself if he is willing to put forth the kind of effort, nurture the kind of sensitivity, and adhere to the kind of discipline that will enable him to speak the truth. His understanding of himself as a user of words will have to be guided by his personal loyalty to the Truth, rather than by an affection for the sound

[7] Copyright 1956 Christian Century Foundation. Reprinted by permission from *The Christian Century*.

of his own voice and the turn of his favorite phrases. Certainly we would hope that this quality would be one of those criteria by which a man's readiness to be a minister could be judged.

If the Protestant minister is to be a man of truth, he must also be one who performs concrete, personal acts of witness himself. One of the key ideas which distinguishes the work of the pastor is the idea that he is set free by a church to work full-time at concerns that others can only work at part-time. When this concept is taken seriously by ministers, it has an important implication for the ministry. The minister is thus liberated to get involved in some activities and organizations that take talent and time and, most important, have significant and important goals. He is not set free to waste his time. He is not liberated just to equip others, not just to get others to work. He is also set free to act as an individual Christian person. Because of the work of Martin Luther King and other Christian ministers in the South, the image of a *witnessing* ministry was dramatically created. Because a Methodist minister escorted his young daughter to school in Louisiana in the face of a jeering, hating mob, the image of the minister as an *acting Christian man* was brought into sharp focus. In less dramatic ways, too, every Protestant minister should think of himself as set free to act in his community as a witnessing Christian. Preferably he should get involved in the neglected or unpopular causes of his town or city—work with prisoners in the local jail, slum work, delinquency problems, or alcoholics. With groups such as these, he has a remarkable opportunity to demonstrate "pure" Christian love, for neither he nor his church will gain many new members nor public prestige from such efforts.

It is obvious, too, that the minister is free to act in a loving and concerned way at the time of trouble and tragedy. We have been critical at many points throughout this book of the Protestant ministry, but it is important that we recognize one

123

fact: in spite of all the shortcomings of organization, form, and personality that churches and their pastors demonstrate, there has been considerable redemptive work taking place in the church through the efforts of Christian ministers. No better example of this can be cited than the tender counseling and guidance which pastors from churches have given to persons who have sought their help. Here is an aspect of the Protestant ministry every pastor ought to perpetuate—the desire to help persons with their problems.

Thus, pastoral work as it is usually conceived—that is, visiting the sick, the shut-in, the lonely, the disgruntled, and the bereaved—should continue to be a major responsibility of a minister. Indeed, if he is truly a part of the Christian *koinonia* which he seeks to help build, he could scarcely not get involved in these efforts. The minister should do much of the pastoral work that needs to be done, not because it is his job, but because it is every Christian's job. He will undoubtedly end up doing more than other people because he is financially set free and has more time. He must be careful and not distort this role by doing all the calling or by failing to get other Christians to realize their responsibilities in this regard.

The man of truth, then, is a person very much like some of the best ministers we have known: a kind, sensitive, concerned individual who cares for people. Realistically, what conscious self-image the minister has in his mind at this point probably makes little difference. If a pastor is seriously concerned, sincerely sympathetic, and sincerely responsive to the needs of persons, the people with whom he comes into contact will sense his sincerity. If he is not, then regardless of how he thinks of himself, his real attitude will probably break through.

Finally the man who chooses the pastorate must be a man of truth in terms of his dedication. When denominations and ministerial pressure groups concentrate *too much* on bettering the lot of the average pastor, they may well be trading one sickness for another. This we must not do. Included as an integral part of the meaning of the Protestant ministry is the need for personal dedication. As the shorter work week becomes common for more and more Americans, the long work week should remain constant for the minister. His full-time ministry should demand of him his energy, his best talents, his time, and all of his personal resources. He who would be a pastor among Christian people must anticipate only an adequate wage. Perhaps we should think in terms of a *maximum* wage for himself as well as in terms of a *minimum* wage for the minister. The man of truth should assume that more is expected of him than of others, rather than feel he will deserve more material rewards and professional advancements as time goes on.

Sacrifice of different kinds and varying degrees will be expected of men and women in the Protestant ministry. The persons it will take to rejuvenate the Church, to help it find purpose and meaning, to kindle fires of adventure and excitement, to fan the sparks of life that still burn in the ash heaps of many a dying church across the land, are of a very high type indeed. If the Protestant pastorate is to provide a first-rate ministry, it will have to be filled by our first-rate people.

Should the day come when the Protestant ministry is just "one more job," then its condition will be far more serious than it now is. Dedicated, conscientious Christian people surely will be willing to spend themselves even sacrificially in the pastoral ministry *if* they can be convinced that the church at the local level is worth the sacrifices it will take to get the job done. In making this decision every minister—present and future— will have to examine his own motives, his own loyalties, and the depth of his commitment. This is a sobering responsibility, especially for any man or woman who would be a seeker after truth in our time.

chapter 7

The Encounter with Resistance

*Do not concern thyself overmuch about
who is for thee or against thee; but take
care to act so that God will be with thee
in everything that thou doest.*
—THOMAS Á KEMPIS

MANY MEN NOW IN THE MINISTRY WOULD LIKE TO BE DOING A
more effective job of being Christian pastors. Some who have
left the pastorate have done so because they felt helpless and
frustrated in their local situations. They really wanted to serve
God, but they felt so much resistance to a change in the conventional work of a pastor that they left for greener pastures. One
ex-minister, writing anonymously for the *Saturday Evening
Post*, described his feelings upon making the decision to leave
the ministry, in this way:

This was not the ministry to which I had felt a call. Nor did
there appear to be any hope that things would change for the better in my lifetime. Soon I would have a larger family. And, as is
the case with many other ministers who want to quit, I would be
trapped. My life would then be wasted as a recreation director for
what essentially seemed to me to be little more than a U.S.O. for

civilians or a Sunday-morning mutual-admiration society. *Why not quit now, I reasoned, study sociology, then make my life count by taking Christianity into the mainstream of life? I could become a university instructor and be able to influence young minds. Then, sometime, perhaps I would have a chance to enter public service.*[1]

Men are *leaving* the pastorate, in other words, for essentially the same reasons why many qualified potential pastors are turning away from the local church.

There is little doubt that many ministers past, present, and future are eager for something better, but they also feel trapped by the stereotype of the past which repels them. Many men have a strong temptation simply to throw up their hands and say, "What's the use?" "I wanted to be a person," a minister complained, "but my church wants me to be a stuffed shirt. I wanted to be a minister, but my people turned me into a puppet. I wanted to lead my church to serve the world, but I ended up being my church's servant." [2]

While it is true that much of what is wrong with the pastorate is the sickness of the ministry, it is also true that the sickness of local congregations has made the task of an equipping minister more difficult. How can a pastor be a teacher if no one comes to a class to be taught? How can he be a catalyst if people ignore his efforts? How can he concentrate on building a community of persons when a congregation is preoccupied with paying off a building debt? Why be a man of truth when many leading church members delight in the vision of their pastor blessing the most important gatherings in the community as the official prayer-giver? We cannot ignore the fact that there

[1] "Why I Quit the Ministry," by an Anonymous Clergyman, as told to Alfred Balk. Reprinted by special permission of *The Saturday Evening Post*. © 1962 The Curtis Publishing Company.

[2] Roy Pearson, "Don't Blame the Laymen!" *The Pulpit*, November, 1961, p. 7. Copyrighted by The Christian Century Foundation.

is real pressure in almost every congregation to mold ministers into the "status seekers" we described earlier.

This resistance cannot be minimized. It cannot be taken lightly. The reason why Gordon Cosby started his remarkable experiment at the Church of the Savior was simply that he didn't think it was possible for a vital, ministering church to be created in an existing, conventional church situation. So he and his wife started a new church and a new idea. Certainly this much is true: the man who seeks to be an equipping minister in most churches is going to meet resistance. It will take several forms and in many cases it will be kindly resistance, as many Christians sincerely try to be fair with a pastor but instead make his fundamental task more difficult.

One form of resistance the minister often faces is a kind of rigidity and inflexibility which has been solidified over the years in many a local church. It should not be surprising to ministers that it was a preacher who wrote in Ecclesiastes:

> What has been is what will be,
>   and what has been done is what will be done;
>   and there is nothing new under the sun.
>   —Eccl. 1:9 (R.S.V.)

That preacher must have just come from a meeting of his official board! There is often an underlying attitude—bordering on the phenomenal—that many men and women have toward money, ideas, suggestions, and projects when they are considered in the context of the church. You can almost hear the trapdoors in people's heads slamming shut as minds are closed. Men who in business will deal in thousands of dollars and take calculated risks with huge investments will debate extensively the purchase of a new typewriter for the church office. Women who will arise at 5:30 A.M. to prepare bean salad and cole slaw for a money-raising luncheon (that will net their group $22.33) will spontaneously balk at the idea of going on an all-day retreat. Taking a youth group to a slum in a nearby city may be vetoed by the comment, "We ought to take care of our own first." If a work camp is arranged in one's own city, it is resisted by the comment, accompanied by the nodding of many heads, "If those people weren't such drunkards, they could take care of their own problems." What has been is what will be, and what has been done is what will be done, and many ministers privately feel that there is a secret conspiracy on the part of church members to make sure that nothing new be tried under the sun.

A second form of resistance that is sometimes encountered is the tendency that many good church members have to put a minister up on a pedestal. We are all keenly aware of the double standards which exist in the church, and to some extent they will always be present. One of the most frequently cited reasons why young men do not go into the pastoral ministry is that "they are not good enough." It is, of course, big news when a minister gets a speeding ticket or a divorce. For anyone else it is merely part of life's little trials. Morally, ministers are on pedestals because they have, by virtue of their vocations, gone on record as having taken the Christian faith seriously.

Some pastors have overreacted to this tendency and have become "regular guys" who trade one trouble for another. Others may want to be taken down from their pedestals because they subconsciously feel they are entitled to a few sins for therapeutic purposes. However, the real burden of the minister's having been placed on a pedestal is simply that a false separation hinders the religious search of the Christian community. When the man-to-man, person-to-person relationship in study, worship, discussion, and work is changed into a man-to-pedagogue, person-to-"parson" relationship, *searching* for the truth sometimes becomes merely a *waiting* for the "Answer Man" to *give* the truth. The minister who is sincerely eager to help people get at the deep problems of existence in a study group may find that many in the group are shy about admitting in front of their pastor that they don't pray or that they really feel Mrs. Jones's Sunday-school class is not very edifying. When a minister is placed on a pedestal, this seemingly kind and respectful attitude hinders a minister in his work—if he sincerely is seeking to equip people for their ministries.

Another form of resistance which the conscientious minister often faces is an opposite one. Many Christians are in total agreement with the idea that a minister should be a "servant" and not a status seeker. However, what they mean is that he should be *their* servant and not necessarily Christ's. By servant, they mean "hired help," a religious handyman, someone who is to come running whenever they call. Protestants, many of them, are in the habit of letting George, the pastor, do whatever trivial work there is that comes the church's way.

A satirical article in *Pulpit* magazine illustrates this tendency of some congregations to pass the buck and let the minister handle whatsoever is good and true and trivial.

You may have heard of the old Scottish lady who referred to a young man as obviously fitted for the ministry, because he was a "right harmless laddie." . . . For many a layman this is the picture of the ideal minister. He must be "spiritual," by which is meant otherworldly. He must be willing to run errands and do whatever the church cannot get anybody else to do. He must speak of matters so esoteric and general that no man will be stabbed in his conscience or troubled in his mind. Let preachers believe all is well while the practical men go about their business. The minister cannot do any harm at a wedding or a funeral, and if he can tell some pretty good stories after dinner for free, that will be fine.[3]

[3] G. Hobab Kish, "The Mourners Bench," *The Pulpit*, October, 1961, p. 21. Copyrighted by The Christian Century Foundation.

Many a man would be glad to be an "equipping minister," but by the time he hauls the youth group to the picnic and hunts up the decorations for the Christmas party and runs next door to the church to see if the potted plant for Sunday's services is still fit to use and responds to the grapevine-delivered call that Mrs. Jones is a little miffed because he hasn't dropped in to "see how she is getting on"—by the time these matters are taken care of, the pastor's day is half-gone and he is deeply involved in self-analysis, wondering whether, instead of having gone to seminary, he should have gone to an agricultural college and lettered in track. These, he may think, would have prepared him better for the expectations of the people he "serves."

Such forms of resistance are seldom open and clear-cut, either to the pastor or the congregations. When we try to put our finger on the source of the rigidity, the setting apart of the pastor, and the trivial demands which characterize the barriers a conscientious minister faces, we find no simple, easy matter. We are confronted by a more or less inarticulate attitude of mind. The resistance is real, however, and it is understandable to many of us in the ministry why some of our sincere and conscientious colleagues have left the pastorate, and why some good candidates are choosing other vocations in which to spend their fruitful years.

It is understandable, we say, but not necessarily excusable. The key fact which pastors and lay ministers must face about the contemporary church is that it is not the gathered community of Christians it is often assumed to be. The congregation—that is, the church roll which includes both nominal and active members—is itself a mission field. For a pastor in our time to give up because he meets this resistance is comparable to a missionary returning home from a mission field upon discovering that the natives were not already Christians. On our church roles are large numbers of genial pagans, worldly men of success, and people who for years have been using their religion to justify what they wanted to do anyway. Many times they are even leaders in the church.

Roy Pearson, dean of the Andover Newton Theological School, is keenly aware of the resistance to a vital ministry, but he offers a direct and pointed suggestion as to the appropriate attitude for a Christian minister in our day.

The man of only ordinary imagination and ability finds it more feasible to *maintain* an institution than to *lead* it. "Doing what comes naturally," he conveys the impression that he is doing what a minister ought to be doing; conveying that impression, he creates a stereotype in the minds of his people; seeing himself reflected in his people's consequent expectations, he does not like what he sees; and not wanting to blame himself, he blames his people. . .

The minister who thinks that his people's ignorance and sin disqualify them for his ministry is incredibly naïve about himself and abysmally unaware of the meaning of ministry. The situation he deplores is the reason for his being. It is the substance of his calling, the material for his labor, the justification for his salary. His real ground for anxiety ought not to be that he is too good for his people —too pure, too wise, or too able: it ought to be that however small or unimpressive his charge, it is too big for his thin talents and too important for his meager intelligence.[4]

Encountering resistance is part of the minister's Christian task. Ours is a sophisticated age, and we can seldom expect to do battle with devils who face us with flags flying, clearly identified as the enemy. They are in disguise—the disguise of traditions, good intentions, ignorance, rigidity, and many misconceptions of what the church really is.

How, then, do we meet resistance? How do we get started toward the goal of being the pastor to ministers in the churches?

[4] Pearson, *op. cit.*, p. 8.

If and when the pastor can see for himself what the ministry ought to be, how can he get the people with whom his life is intricately involved to share the meaning of ministry and the meaning of the church that he has?

We need to emphasize that *being* an equipping minister will itself be an effective way of combating resistance. We have already said, for example, that the presence of *koinonia* makes honesty and forthrightness easier and, consequently, some changes in the attitude of church members possible. If the pastor really does function as a catalyst, a wider ministry will come into existence whose effects are noticeable and self-justifying. When a minister is an effective teacher, the word will get around and greater response will be forthcoming. And when the pastor lives the kind of life and demonstrates that he *is* a man of truth, resistance is encountered in those moments.

However, more than this alone will be necessary. While there is no definite, clear-cut strategy which guarantees the successful overcoming of resistance, some guideposts for action can be spelled out. The first of these is keynoted by the word "persistence." The nature of the church and the work of the ministry will have to be preached, discussed, presented, debated, and reconsidered over and over again. A token effort will not help people see how serious this matter is. The idea of what a ministering church is is not grasped the first time around, or the second, or—by many people—even the third or fourth times. When enough people don't appear at the first series of classes in "The Meaning of the Church," a new series will have to be scheduled at a new time under a new title that deals with the same subject. When a member of the congregation leads the worship service and can't be heard by the ladies on the back row, be sure the next man can project his voice or has access to a loudspeaker system. If the official board members cannot afford to go away for a weekend retreat because it costs too

133

much, less expensive arrangements will have to be made or a subsidy will have to be included for it in the next church budget.

Persistence in this effort will require time; this is obvious. It is also true that there will be times when compromise is necessary. When called upon suddenly to bless the food, the blessing will have to be said and a point about the priesthood of all believers made later. We must learn the difference between a strategic withdrawal and losing the war. *We must be willing to compromise but not to be compromised.* The mold with which a minister must contend is not shattered and then replaced suddenly by a new one. It is bent here and there, heated over a slow fire, and gradually reshaped into something better. Patience is mandatory. A sense of humor and the ability to laugh at one's self will have to be developed. But the goal of what the church is and what the work of the ministry ought to be must always be in the back of a pastor's mind, and this standard can never be compromised.

A second guidepost for the encounter with resistance is the word "experiment." Nothing succeeds like success, and it is always amazing to learn how many people were "for" a somewhat venturesome project *after* it has succeeded. An encouraging fact is that many projects which can be tried successfully are not really daring but seem to be in the context of the usual church program. For example, in our own community the project was undertaken to open in a downtown location a non-denominational, non-profit religious bookstore for laymen. From a business point of view, very little risk was involved. The rent was inexpensive, even though the location was a good one. The store was staffed by volunteer help, so no salaries had to be paid. Equipment needs were simple, and everything was readily available for use on loan. Utilities cost practically nothing, and a number of donors came forward with what little capital was needed. A small investigation even revealed that all the books we needed could be obtained on consignment. Yet to many people this project has appeared to be as courageous as the Crusades and as daring as the initial flight of the Wright brothers.

It *is* a different project, of course, and a number of problems which had not been anticipated have become apparent. Yet, it is a success; a co-operative program of outreach—the spreading of Christian ideas through books—is being carried on. However, the significant point is the change in the psychological attitude that has been taking place because of the project. Those directly involved are enthusiastic and the degree of excitement generated by them has been contagious. We are able to have something real and tangible to which we can point and say, "This is what we mean by being creative Christians." A similar project is being conducted by the Aldersgate Methodist Church near Cleveland, and there are undoubtedly countless other attempts which have nothing to do with bookstores that could be made in community after community across the country. The project itself must be worthwhile and valuable, but the by-product of enthusiasm and adventure is itself worth the effort.

In a general way Elton Trueblood has given us the reason why pilot projects are frequently the means of changing an attitude of reluctance and timidity.

There are times, of course, when a degree of caution is really wise, but there are countless other times when it is damaging to the spirit of adventure which our world so sorely needs and which is relatively scarce. What needs stressing now is the spirit which sees the need and proposes to follow at once something that involves a promise of help. The awful futility of our time cannot be overstated; the worst thing we can do is to do nothing. Accordingly we require the emergence of a bold and experimental spirit which is willing to gamble, in our desperate situation, on a fundamental

Christian insight. There are always difficulties in the way of any course, as there were in the way proposed by St. Paul or by George Fox, but we are glad today that these bold spirits were not balked by the fact that such difficulties existed. They could not see all the way, and they were aware that the feelings of some people would be hurt if they should persist in the intended course, but this did not stop them. There are times when patience becomes a positive vice, closely associated with cowardice. It is good to realize that, while in some situations there is a grace of patience, in other situations there is a grace of impatience.[5]

Persistence and experimentation are both necessary and required guideposts in the encounter with resistance in which the minister who wishes to serve God will find himself.

A third guidepost, closely related to our emphasis upon experimentation, is highlighted by the word "seeker." A continual distraction to the work of the pastor is the ever-present success standard of statistics. The minister is probably as guilty of being a victim of this distraction as the layman, the evidence for which can be observed at almost any ministers' meeting in those moments when the pastors trade the usual question, "How are you doing?" In translation this means very simply, "How many did you have out Sunday?" Yet as the *ministering* success of the Church of the Savior has dramatically indicated, the important question is not *how many?* but *who?* By the grace of God and the work of the Holy Spirit, there are some in practically all churches who are "seekers," who no more fit the stereotype of the resisting layman than some pastors fit the unfortunate stereotype of the minister. These people can be invaluable allies in the encounter with resistance.

There is no set group of people who automatically will join the pastor in the front lines of the encounter. They are not

[5] D. Elton Trueblood, *Alternative to Futility* (New York: Harper & Row, 1948), pp. 106-7.

all in one Sunday-school class nor in responsible positions in the church. They are not of one age group, although a high percentage of the "seekers" will probably be found in the wide range of young adulthood. They may be long-time members or they may have come into the church because of the kind of fellowship they have seen. Their primary identifying mark is seen in their response to the program that an equipping minister nurtures. The "seekers" are those who are not satisfied with the clichés of Christendom and the dogmas which they don't understand. They may be tired of serving chili suppers, and they frequently are tired of using their church time for social activities. In one suburban Congregational church a group of young adults actually asked the minister of their church to start a study group in which serious questions of the Christian faith might be examined. There is reason to think, furthermore, that the suburbs (where local Christianity is usually thought of as especially shallow and superficial) may have many more "seekers" than anyone now believes. Suburbanites do not need the church for picnics, parties, and recreation because they have their own resources for leisure and entertainment. There are probably many who are ready to respond—if a challenging and serious program is offered.

The "seekers" merit the special attention of the equipping minister. True, a minister must be pastor of all the congregation, both the interested and those who couldn't care less, but to get help in the cause of the church he will necessarily have to tell his story to those who will listen—and help. Jesus Christ did not reach everyone, and while he occasionally appeared before large groups, the vast bulk of his time was spent with the twelve. *To think* that failure is indicated by a lack of numbers is the real failure, not the fact of the small numerical response itself. Numerical success is a by-product, not a goal.

Finally, the denomination of which the local church is a part

137

may be a help in the remolding of the pastor's and the people's work. The amount of help a denomination will give a pastor in meeting local resistance and breaking old stereotypes will vary greatly from denomination to denomination, and often even within a single denomination, depending upon the officials involved. Sadly, it is true that part of the unhappy situation of the Protestant ministry in America is tied up with more than local factors. Church structures often reflect the weaknesses of the local church, and denominations at times seem to be seriously compounding and worsening the predicament of the church and the ministry. The way that some denominations have seen fit to "relocate" some ministers who rock the boat is one illustration. The pressure in others for the local minister to produce statistical success in order to increase the glory of the denomination is another. The fact that many denominational officials are competitors who have worked their way "up the ladder" and who seek to protect their vested interests partially accounts for the failure of local churches and denominations to be on the firing line in the great social and ethical issues of the day. We would be naïve if we thought the trouble were simply a local dilemma.

However there are denominational leaders and there are denominational programs which can be helpful to the pastor in his encounter with resistance. We have already referred to some of the seminars, training programs, and retreats which denominations provide that will aid the pastor in his task of equipping others for their ministry. More than a few times, also, a bishop or a superintendent or an executive secretary has lent his influence and given his blessing to the creative and prophetic work of a local pastor.

This, of course, is a two-way street. The way we change the national scene is by changing local units. There is no church unless there are local churches. The denomination exists as a help and a stimulus to the local church, but the local church and the local pastor have a ministry that must be directed toward the denomination. Some of the battles against resistance in the local situation will one day be won after some of the battles have been fought in denominational headquarters. "The stained-glass jungle" is a jungle that exists on more than one plateau. The encounter with resistance will have to take place at all the points where the underbrush is thickest.

The problems of sterility and rigidity in the church are not the exclusive concern of the pastor. It must ultimately be faced and overcome by Christian congregations as well as in the minds of ministers. It is a vital part of the pastor's task to confront this resistance, and he ought not retreat just because people are not tripping over each other's feet in response to the demands of the gospel as he presents them. Seldom, if ever, has there been a rush of people to take up a cross, and yet this is the call of the New Testament. Interdependence of pastor and people is essential if there will be a renewal of the Christian ministry. Pastors and lay Christians share the guilt for the current distortions within the church, just as they share the responsibility for revitalizing the faith. Initiative and response in Christian work is not only a vertical phenomenon, as the minister pulls the people *up* to him. It is a horizontal relationship as well. Both initiative and response must be shared in Protestantism by Christians, some of whom are pastors and some of whom are not. When this happens, the pastor will know that he is winning the encounter with resistance.

There is no doubt that there needs to be a renewal of the ministry in the church. Strong leadership was the core of the great days of Christian beginnings and of every revival that has taken place since. It will be at the core of whatever dynamic efforts—if any—Christians make now. Conventional leadership will not do, and a conventional ministry for a revitalized church will not be satisfactory. We need the best people we can find to work in the ministry today, and we need an understanding of the ministry worthy of their best dedication.

Young men and women are restless to act positively in our time. They are taking freedom rides, and participating in sit-ins, and joining the Peace Corps, and some are looking for significant ways of serving God in the pastorate. Those who really want to serve God in our day really want to serve *him,* not an institution, not a set of customs, and certainly not a church that has lost its sense of destiny. There is work to be done. It is real, significant, challenging, demanding, time-consuming Christian work. It is work that needs to be done by leaders and followers, by those who teach, and those who learn, by those who inspire, and those who then come alive.

There is work to be done. It is high time we get at it, for it is our Father's business we are now neglecting.

Index

141

76